AI and ML-Driven Cybersecurity

While the Industrial Internet of Things (IIoT) and Wireless Sensor Networks (WSNs) continue to redefine industrial infrastructure, the need for proactive, intelligent, and scalable cybersecurity solutions has never been more pressing. This book provides a hands-on, research-driven guide to building, deploying, and understanding machine learning models tailored for securing IIoT and WSN environments.

Whether you're a student, researcher, or professional, this book takes you through the full data science lifecycle—from data collection and EDA to model development and deployment—with a special focus on real-world attack detection, anomaly analysis, and predictive defense strategies.

You'll learn:

- How to run a cybersecurity-focused exploratory data analysis (EDA)
- Step-by-step model design, training, and evaluation for threat detection
- Building and deploying web-based AI cybersecurity solutions
- Practical use of Python
- Visualizing attacks and insights to drive decision-making
- Future trends include Edge AI, federated learning, and zero-trust security

This book is intended for cybersecurity professionals working in industrial or smart environments, including smart cities, aerospace, manufacturing, etc. It is also a valuable resource for data scientists and ML engineers applying AI to security, industrial engineers, and university students and educators in computer science, data science, and security. **Build secure, data-driven defenses for the next generation of connected systems—start here.**

AI and ML-Driven Cybersecurity
Industrial IoT and WSN with Python Scripting

Atdhe Buja

CRC Press
Taylor & Francis Group
Boca Raton London New York

CRC Press is an imprint of the
Taylor & Francis Group, an **informa** business

Designed cover image: Shutterstock

First edition published 2026
by CRC Press
2385 NW Executive Center Drive, Suite 320, Boca Raton FL 33431

and by CRC Press
4 Park Square, Milton Park, Abingdon, Oxon, OX14 4RN

CRC Press is an imprint of Taylor & Francis Group, LLC

© 2026 Atdhe Buja

ISBN: 978-1-041-05039-1 (hbk)
ISBN: 978-1-041-05141-1 (pbk)
ISBN: 978-1-003-63151-4 (ebk)

DOI: 10.1201/9781003631514

Typeset in Adobe Casion
by Newgen Publishing UK

Dedicated to my family, Donika (wife), and Oda and Jeta (daughters)

A great thank you to my reviewers, Prof. Akihiko Mutoh and Blent Kurtalani

Contents

VIII   CONTENTS

About the Author

Atdhe Buja, Commonwealth University of Pennsylvania, Bloomsburg. Atdhe Buja is an assistant professor in the Department of Computer Science, Math, and Digital Forensics at the Commonwealth University of Pennsylvania, Bloomsburg. He is a world-renowned cybersecurity expert with decades of experience and he is a leader in information technology and Industrial IoT cybersecurity. His work has been presented at several conferences, including FIRST cybersecurity, Hackathons, Astana IT University, Balkan Cybersecurity DCAF, Japan, cybersecurity Workshops, Safer Internet Day, etc. He has participated many times in DEFCON, and he is a well-known expert on CERT teams, having developed and built CERT in academia and in the private sector (ICT Academy CERT). He has held a variety of roles in the cybersecurity industry, and has developed several video courses for the industry and the ICT Academy on VAPT, incident handling, SOC, Pentest, machine learning introduction, IoT security, attack scenarios and incident response, and cyber systems and network forensics. He leads many research projects for ICT Academy with the Astana International Scientific Complex and the Global Cyber Alliance, developing innovative solutions that leverage machine learning, artificial intelligence, and cybersecurity to meet needs surrounding wireless sensor networks, the Internet of Things, and Industrial IoT.

Figures

Tables

Preface

The prompt advancement of technology has significantly transformed industrial settings, establishing the Industrial Internet of Things (IIoT) and wireless sensor networks (WSNs) as a basic component of Industry 4.0. With this transformation comes an urgent need for robust, intelligent cybersecurity mechanisms. This book provides a practical and research-informed journey into securing IIoT and WSN environments using artificial intelligence, machine learning, and predictive analytics.

The chapters are structured to guide readers from foundational concepts to real-world application, beginning with data understanding and advancing through model design, development, deployment, and reflection on emerging challenges. Each chapter includes hands-on practices, visualizations, and insights drawn from field research, aiming to equip students, practitioners, and researchers with the tools to build and apply AI-powered cybersecurity solutions.

Whether you are a learner seeking to understand cybersecurity's role in smart systems or a professional building an intelligent defense, this book offers both the theoretical grounding and practical roadmap needed to navigate the future of IIoT and WSN security.

This book aims to equip professionals, researchers, and students with the knowledge to protect IIoT settings, fostering innovation while mitigating risks. Arching over foundational principles and modern approaches provides a valuable resource for securing the future of industrial systems.

1

CYBERSECURITY
FOR IIoT AND WSNs

1.1 Cybersecurity for IIoT and WSNs

The Industrial Internet of Things, known as IIoT, expresses itself as a subset of Internet of Things (IoT) technology within the usage of the industrial sectors and applications. In the modern digital overview, the integration of the Industrial Internet of Things (IIoT) and wireless sensor networks (WSNs) has changed many industrial sectors, including manufacturing, healthcare, and energy. This enhancement of these technologies has introduced a significant level of efficiency, automation, and data-driven decision-making. Nevertheless, these developments and evolutions have brought about cybersecurity challenges that need to be addressed to ensure the protection of sensitive information and the integrity of industrial systems. Cybersecurity for IIoT and WSNs demands a thorough approach to protect these networks from potential threats and vulnerabilities; nevertheless, it requires a defense. As we deep dive into this chapter, we will investigate basic concepts, types of cybersecurity, and practices to mitigate risks related to these evolved technologies.

1.2 Types of Cybersecurity

Cybersecurity is mainly categorized into many types, focused on various views of network and information protection. Network security demands security measures or controls to protect the integrity and utility of the network infrastructure. Information security is about protecting data from threats, unauthorized access, or changes.

DOI: 10.1201/9781003631514-1   1

Application security points to defending software applications from risks and threats. Operational security means processes that handle and safeguard data assets, although physical security makes sure that the protection of hardware and physical infrastructure is maintained.

Additionally, the presentation of IIoT and WSNs as technologies has led the way to the emergence of certain cybersecurity types guided to handle the distinctive challenges caused by these integrated systems. For example, the security of endpoints at IIoT systems is most important, as it secures many devices connected to industrial infrastructures. Likewise, cloud security is more and more important as IIoT and WSN application solutions are now built and based on cloud services for their many better features. As we expand further into the complexities of cybersecurity for IIoT and WSNs, it is crucial to understand and implement effective cybersecurity practices. The practices include and aim at the identification, assessment, and mitigation of potential threats and vulnerabilities to ensure the stable protection of industrial infrastructure and systems.

1.3   Cybersecurity Practices

First, let's start with a very concise and important explanation of cybersecurity practices. Primarily, practices of cybersecurity can be carried out through three main activities, which are vulnerability assessment, penetration testing, also known as pentest, and risk assessment. Further, in this part of the section, we will elaborate in detail on the common steps of those activities.

1.3.1   *Vulnerability Assessment*

Vulnerability assessment is known as a crucial activity in noticing and mitigating any potential lack or gaps within the IIoT and WSN infrastructures. Through an organized process of scanning and examining systems to unearth security gaps, organizations benefit from proactively mitigating vulnerabilities before they are exploited by hackers or any malicious actors. Systematic vulnerability assessments are important to preserve the security posture of IIoT and WSN installations. Table 1.1 shows the process of vulnerability assessment as a cybersecurity practice activity. The table introduces each step in

Table 1.1 Vulnerability Assessment – Detailed Steps and Description

STEP	DESCRIPTION
Identify Assets	Listing all critical assets within the IIoT and WSN environments
Threat Detection	Identification of potential threats
Risk Evaluation	Shows a risk matrix that evaluates the likelihood and impact of identified threats
Scan and Analyze	A scanning tool that systematically scans the network and devices for vulnerabilities
Prioritization	Prioritization chart to rank vulnerabilities based on their severity and potential impact
Mitigation	Implementation of mitigation strategies such as patches, updates, and security controls

the process and includes an expanded explanation that enhances the understanding of this crucial cybersecurity practice activity.

1.3.2 Penetration Testing

Penetration testing of well-known cyber-attack simulations makes a major contribution to securing the Industrial Internet of Things (IIoT) and wireless sensor networks (WSNs). These technologies are extensive in industrial infrastructure environments, providing advanced functionality such as connectivity and operational efficiency. Nevertheless, complexity and a diverse nature bring risks to cybersecurity. In the setting of IIoT, penetration testing necessitates the simulation of cyber-attacks to point out vulnerabilities within the infrastructure of industrial devices, control systems, and communication protocols. This process began with a comprehensive mapping of the IIoT network, identifying all connected devices and their related communication protocols. Penetration testers utilize their expertise through various tools to examine for gaps, including default credentials, unpatched firmware, open ports, and unsecured data transmissions. Then, through the step of the process in which exploitation occurs, vulnerabilities in a controlled setting (sandbox), penetration testers can evaluate the potential impact of a particular cyber-attack on industrial operations.

On the other hand, for wireless sensor networks, the penetration testing process centers on the distinctive challenges caused by their commonly limited resources and frequent installation in harsh or remote environments. Penetration testers assess the security posture of sensor nodes, communication links, and data aggregation points. They assess the strength of the encryption protocols, the capability of the authentication mechanisms, and the persistence of the network against jamming and spoofing attacks. In addition, testing serves to identify vulnerabilities in network management protocols and the likelihood of unauthorized access to sensor data. The outcome gained from the penetration testing process in IIoT and WSN settings is crucial for designing the application of effective mitigation strategies. Time is precious if you need to identify and mitigate security weaknesses before hackers can exploit them, this will give organizations benefits to advance their Cybersecurity posture. This proactive mindset and culture are vital for defending sensitive industrial processes and data, ensuring the integrity, availability, and safety of critical infrastructure.

1.3.3   Risk Assessment

Risk assessment is an elemental cybersecurity activity for the Industrial Internet of Things (IIoT) and wireless sensor networks (WSNs). This process requires identifying, assessing, and prioritizing potential threats to these technologies, which are vital in industrial settings. Given the intricacy and variety of IIoT and WSN settings, a thorough risk assessment is important for the defense of critical infrastructure. At first, the risk assessment process includes a comprehensive inventory of all assets within the IIoT and WSN infrastructure or domain. This consists of documentation for all devices, sensors, communication protocols, and industrial control systems. By apprehension of the overall network, cybersecurity professionals can identify gaps where vulnerability may exist. Then, the assessment examines the potential threats and vulnerabilities related to IIoT and WSNs. Specifically, for IIoT, this includes risks to unpatched firmware, weak authentication mechanisms, and unsecured communication channels. For WSNs, issues include limited device resources, liability for physical tampering, and potential for denial-of-service attacks.

Preceding the identification of vulnerabilities, the risk assessment process includes evaluating the potential impact of these vulnerabilities on industrial operations. This step is important in prioritizing risks that would need immediate attention over ones which could be mitigated later. The utilization of a risk matrix and severity scoring points toward the visualization and ranking of these threats and potential cyber-attacks. Also, risk assessment in IIoT and WSN environments should consider the advancements in cyber-threats and -attacks. Regular monitoring and updating of the risk assessment are called for to transform with or adjust to new vulnerabilities and emerging attack vectors. This proactive mindset and culture make sure that organizations are aware and ready to protect against cyber-attacks. The outcome of the risk assessment process apprises the development and implementation of strong mitigation strategies. This proactive attitude concerning risk management advanced the cybersecurity posture of industrial environments, protecting the integrity, availability, and safety of critical infrastructure.

1.4 Summary

This chapter talks about the application of mitigation strategies to advance cybersecurity posture. Penetration testing simulates cyber-attacks to identify vulnerabilities in the Industrial Internet of Things (IIoT) and wireless sensor networks (WSNs). The results guide the development of effective mitigation strategies. Risk assessment identifies, evaluates, and prioritizes potential threats to IIoT and WSNs.

1.5 Key Terms

- Penetration Testing
- Industrial Internet of Things (IIoT)
- Wireless Sensor Networks (WSNs)
- Cybersecurity
- Vulnerabilities
- Risk Assessment
- Mitigation Strategies
- Communication Protocols
- Authentication Mechanisms
- Encryption Protocols
- Network Management Protocols
- Denial-of-Service Attacks
- Risk Matrix
- Severity Scoring

1.6   Review Questions

1. What are the two key components of a Risk Assessment?
   Identification of threats and vulnerabilities and evaluation of their impact and likelihood.

2. Name one popular resource for web application security.
   OWASP (Open Web Application Security Project).

3. What is the purpose of Mitigation Strategies?
   To reduce or eliminate the impact of identified risks.

4. Which organization provides guidelines and best practices for cybersecurity, including Risk Assessment?
   NIST (National Institute of Standards and Technology).

5. What are Authentication Mechanisms used for?
   They are used to verify the identity of users and devices.

6. Name a database that helps organizations identify and address cybersecurity vulnerabilities.
   CVE (Common Vulnerabilities and Exposures).

7. What is the role of Encryption Protocols?
   To protect data by converting it into a secure format that is unreadable without the decryption key.

8. Which online resource offers news, analysis, and research on information security?
   CSO Online.

9. What are Denial-of-Service Attacks designed to do?
   Disrupt the normal functioning of a network or service by overwhelming it with a flood of illegitimate requests.

10. Which resource provides a knowledge base of adversary tactics and techniques?
    MITRE ATT&CK®.

11. What does a Risk Matrix help assess?
    The severity and likelihood of various risks need to be assessed for their mitigation.

1.7   Suggested Websites

- OWASP (Open Web Application Security Project) – [http://owasp.org]: A comprehensive resource for web application security, offering tools and documentation on various security vulnerabilities and best practices for mitigation.

- CVE (Common Vulnerabilities and Exposures) – [http://cve.org]: A database of publicly disclosed cybersecurity vulnerabilities to help organizations identify and address potential risks.
- NIST (National Institute of Standards and Technology) – [www.nist.gov]: Provides guidelines, standards, and best practices for cybersecurity, including risk assessment and mitigation strategies.
- SANS Institute – [www.sans.org]: This offers extensive resources on cybersecurity, including detailed guides on penetration testing, risk assessment, and vulnerability management.
- MITRE ATT&CK® – [https://attack.mitre.org]: A knowledge base of adversary tactics and techniques based on real-world observations, aiding in the understanding and mitigation of threats.
- CSO Online – [www.csoonline.com]: A source for news, analysis, and research on information security and risk management.
- Cybersecurity & Infrastructure Security Agency (CISA) – [www.cisa.gov]: Provides information and tools to enhance the security and resilience of the nation's critical infrastructure.

2

DATA SOURCES FOR PREDICTIVE CYBERSECURITY

2.1 Data Sources for Predictive Cybersecurity

Through understanding the sources and types of data available, we can use them for the mitigation of cyberthreats. Internal data sources are acquired from within the organization and consist of logs from servers, network devices, and security systems. These logs bring sensitive information on user activities, access examples, and potential security breaches. Also, internal databases and application data provide a wealth of information on the performance of the system and user interactivity. External data sources appear from outside the organization and are, to the same degree, essential. They include threat intelligence feeds, which offer real-time updates on emerging threats and vulnerabilities. Open-source intelligence (OSINT) also provides a beneficial perception of potential security risks and threat actor behaviors. The potential of predictive cybersecurity lies in the incorporation of both internal and external data sources. In unison with the data streams, industrial organizations can establish a thorough view of their security posture. This comprehensive direction ensures more correct threat detection and proactive defense strategies.

Ensuring the quality and governance of data is important. Organizations should implement strong data management practices to maintain the accuracy, integrity, and reliability of their data sources, including continuous audits, data cleaning, and compliance with regulatory standards. As technology progresses, the same way data sources are used for predictive cybersecurity. The ascent of the Internet of Things (IoT) and the growing application of cloud services present

DOI: 10.1201/9781003631514-2

new data streams that need to be monitored and analyzed further. Remaining alongside the emerging direction is vital for maintaining a proactive security posture.

An interesting example of an internal data source for predictive cybersecurity in the Industrial Internet of Things (IIoT) and wireless sensor networks (WSNs) is the application of honeypots. Honeypots are trap systems or endpoints designed to imitate original systems and lure hackers and malicious actors. Doing this makes sure organizations monitor and analyze attackers' actions without taking risks on systems. In the background of IIoT, honeypots are applicable to simulate a vulnerable part of the infrastructure, including IoT devices or industrial control systems. These simulations draw malicious actors, where tactics, techniques, and procedures (TTPs) are uncovered as they try to break the trap systems. The data collected from these activities offers valuable insight into emerging threats targeting IIoT systems, enabling organizations to implement and advance their security measures proactively. Likewise, in WSN environments, honeypots can be implemented to introduce sensor nodes or gateways within the network. These trap nodes collect details on intrusion acts, including the utilization of exploits, the origin of the attacks, and the activities manifested by malicious actors. Those data are vital for having a clear view of the security posture of WSNs and for designing and developing predictive models that can elevate the identification and mitigation of attacks to a better level. The incorporation of honeypot data sources in combination with internal and external sources enhances the comprehensive predictive cybersecurity framework. By analyzing the pattern and mark outcomes from honeypot activities, organizations can elevate their threat detection algorithms and overall implementation of effective protection.

2.2 Data Science Lifecycle

This chapter will address and guide based on our data science lifecycle roadmap, as shown in Figure 2.1. We will learn involvement and how to use methods and techniques in each activity of the roadmap. Additionally, Figure 2.1 is mainly divided into two phases: data science consulting phase 1 (where we are now) and data science process phase 2 (the next phase after analysis is concluded).

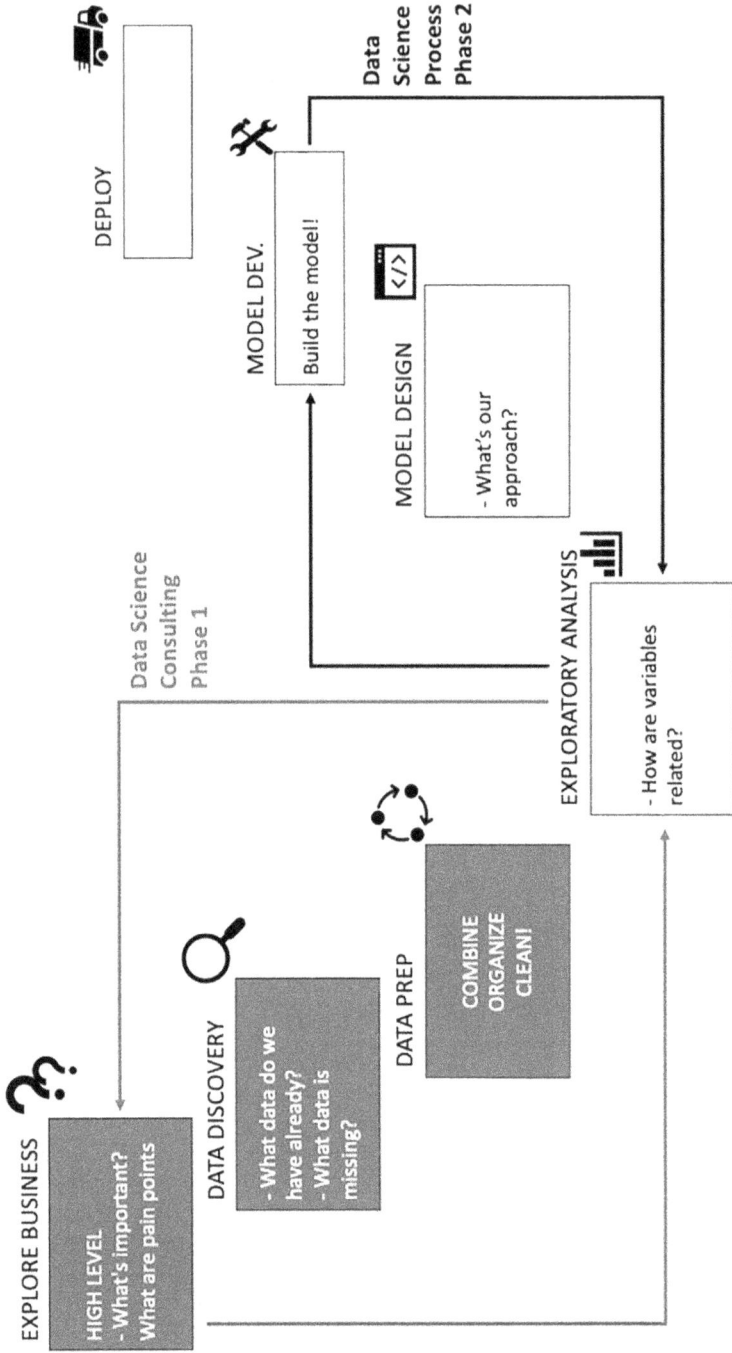

Figure 2.1 Data science lifecycle roadmap.

Details of how to use the data science lifecycle roadmap activities will be provided in the following sections.

2.2.1 Explore Business

The data science lifecycle is a vital component of predictive cybersecurity, enabling organizations to transform raw data into practical insights. The lifecycle contains a variety of key activities, each needing related methodologies and tools to ensure accurate and effective results. Exploring the business background is the first and basic step in the data science lifecycle. This activity includes a comprehensive understanding of the organizational objectives, key performance indicators (KPIs), and key business processes. By engaging ourselves in the business territory, we can better unearth the related problems and opportunities that data science can address. During this activity, cooperation with stakeholders from different divisions and departments is required to collect insights and viewpoints that will build the data science project. This cooperative way makes sure the project is aligned with the strategic objectives of the organization and handles real-world issues.

The first task in exploring the business is to determine the scope and limits of the data science project. This includes pointing out the related data sources, completing the data requirements, and setting clear objectives for the project to achieve. By establishing a fine-defined scope, we can center our attempts in the most sensitive domains and bypass needless complexities. Furthermore, exploring the business background includes running a comprehensive analysis of the actual data infrastructure and resources. This analysis guides us in comprehending the availability, quality, and accessibility of data, which are vital elements for the project's success. It also supplies insights into any possible limitations or constraints that need to be taken care of during the following activities of the lifecycle.

As soon as the business context is clear, we can move to the next activity of the data science lifecycle, which is data discovery. This activity includes identifying, gathering, and organizing related data that will be used for analysis and modeling.

2.2.2   Data Discovery

The data discovery activity is key for identifying, collecting, and organizing the data needed for analysis and modeling. In this activity, we need to address two basic questions:

- What data do we have already?
- What data is missing?

Answering the first question includes inventorying all actual data sources within the industrial organization. This covers internal data (transactional records, customer interactions, system logs, and previously collected honeypot data). Knowing the accessibility and quality of this data, we can decide how it can be beneficial to meeting our project objectives.

The second question needs to identify gaps in our data inventory. This includes knowing external data sources (industry benchmarks, threat intelligence feeds, or honeypot activities), which offer impactful insights into emerging threats. Table 2.1 introduces the approach that guides us to identifying missing data through inventorying all available data for the project.

Succeeding in inventorying available data, and based on objectives for the project to aspire to achieve, we built a dataset. Then, we use a data retrieval process that locates, extracts, and structures data from repositories to build a dataset. For our project, we will use an example dataset named "**IIoT-WSN_CyberThreats**", which can be found at the GitHub repo https://github.com/atdhebuja/IIoT-WSN-Cyber Threat-Dataset with sample data to demonstrate the whole data science lifecycle process of predictive cybersecurity in the Industrial Internet of Things (IIoT) and wireless sensor networks (WSNs). Table 2.2 shows the example dataset fields and a description of the fields, which we will be using over the entire data science lifecycle activities discussed in this book.

Table 2.1   Example of Data Discovery Inventory

NO.	AVAILABLE FIELD	DESCRIPTION OF THE FIELD
1.	id_	Field identifier
2.	@timestamp	Date/timestamp
3.	Protocol	rdp or ss or telnet

Table 2.2 Dataset Fields and Descriptions

FIELD	DESCRIPTION
Timestamp	The time when the attack (or normal event) occurred. Useful for time-series analysis.
Device_ID	Unique identifier for the IIoT/WSN device sending data.
Device_Type	Type of device (e.g., sensor, gateway, actuator).
Protocol	Network communication protocol used (e.g., MQTT, CoAP, HTTP, Modbus, OPC-UA).
Source_IP	The IP address of the source (attacker or normal device).
Destination_IP	The IP address of the target (victim or normal communication node).
Geo_Location	The geographic location of the source device (used for Geo IP analysis).
Packet_Size	Size of the network packet in bytes.
Request_Type	Type of network request (e.g., GET, POST, PUBLISH, SUBSCRIBE).
Payload_Entropy	Measure of randomness in the packet payload (high entropy may indicate an attack).
CPU_Usage (%)	CPU utilization of the IIoT/WSN device at the time of the event.
Memory_Usage (%)	Memory consumption of the device.
Temperature (grade C)	Environmental sensor reading (useful for anomaly detection).
Battery_Level (%)	Battery percentage of the IIoT device.
Malicious_Activity	Whether the activity is malicious or not (1 for attack, 0 for normal).
Attack_Type	If Malicious_Activity = 1, this field classifies the attack (e.g., DDoS, MITM, Spoofing, Injection).

2.2.3 Data Preparation

Data preparation is a key step in the data science lifecycle, including integrating, transforming, organizing, and cleansing data to ensure they are ready for further analysis. This activity includes handling missing values, removing duplicates, and normalizing data. At some point, the data is clean and structured based on our data science project objectives and can be saved in suitable formats like CSV or other data formats such as NoSQL for further exploratory data analysis (EDA).

Figures 2.2–2.11 will introduce the method of running the same environment locally in your PC or laptop by using Jupyter Notebook, which runs Python programming languages.

2.2.4 Exploratory Data Analysis

Exploratory data analysis is a key activity in the data science lifecycle which includes outlining the main characteristics of the dataset, frequently using visual methods. The first goal of EDA is to unearth

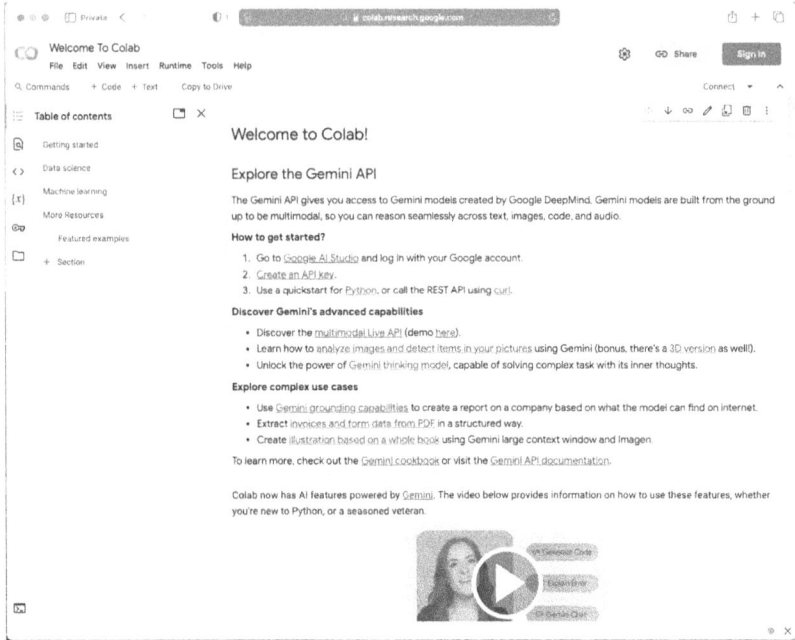

Figure 2.2   Google Colaboratory (Google Colab or Colab) environment overview.

patterns, identify anomalies, test hypotheses, and look at assumptions with the guidance of summary statistics and visual representations. Over this activity, data scientists or researchers attempt to answer different questions, like "How are the variables related?", "Are there any missing values?", and "What are the underlying structures in the data?". Addressing these questions, data scientists or researchers can deep-dive and gain insights into the dataset, which results in activities such as model design, development, and deployment. Chapter 4 details the activity of EDA for cybersecurity insights, including analysis type selection, research question definition, result generation and visualization, and data interpretation.

2.2.5   *Model Design*

Model design activity within the data science lifecycle is a vital step that includes designing a visionary and computational framework to address the research questions and objectives of this project. Our direction to model design is methodically repeated, making sure that the developed

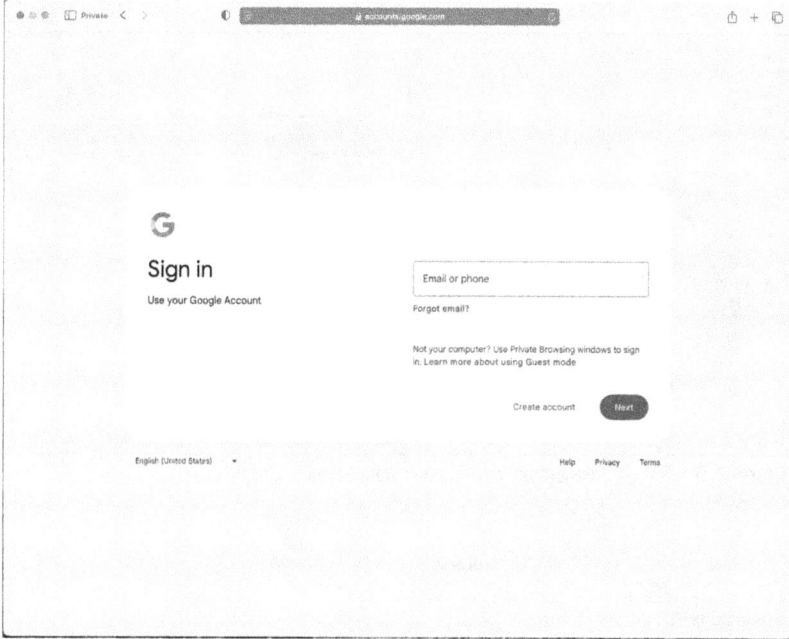

Figure 2.3   Sign in or enter Google Colaboratory.

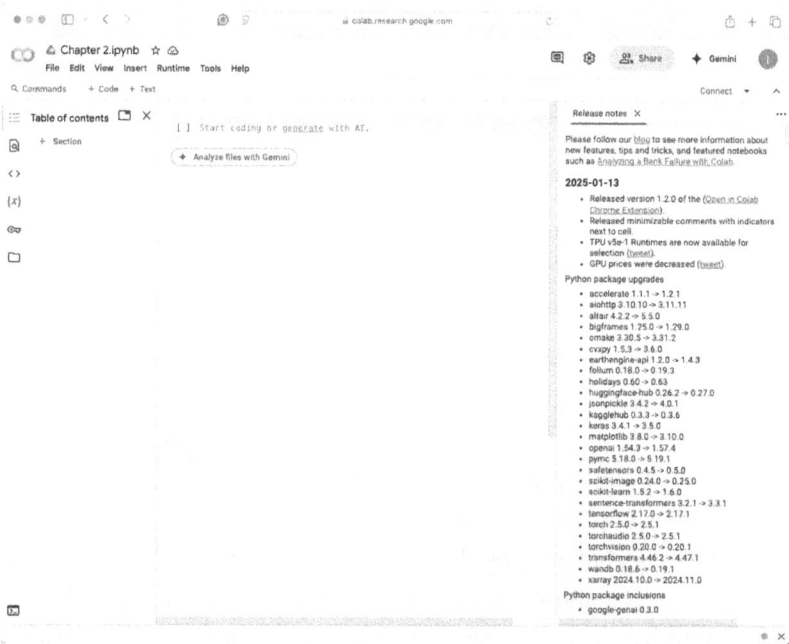

Figure 2.4   Google Colaboratory introduction.

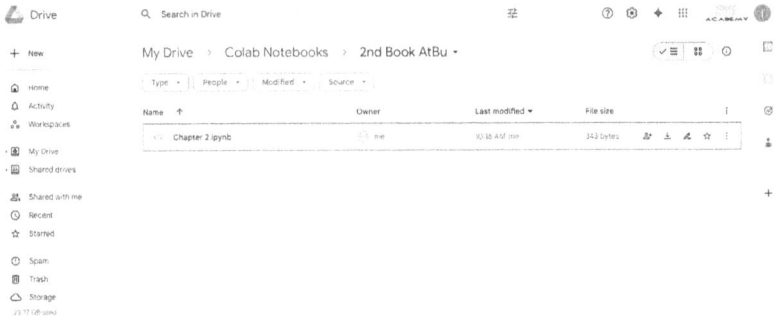

Figure 2.5   Google Colaboratory environment work saved to Google drive.

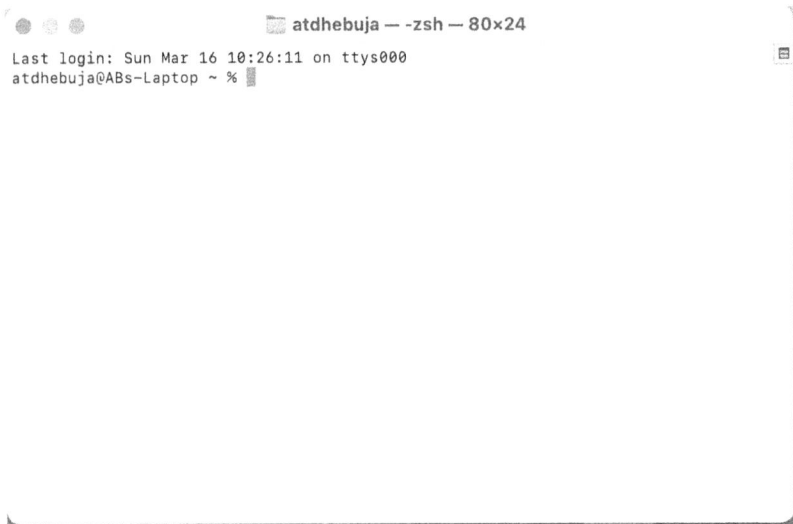

Figure 2.6   Jupyter Notebook environment alternative of Google Colab.

models are strong, extensible, and aligned with the project objectives. Commonly, we begin by choosing suitable algorithms and techniques based on the problem and the type of available data we would work with. This way is chosen by the insight outcome from EDA, where we unearth patterns, anomalies, and relationships within the data. Then, we move on to feature engineering, which includes building new variables or changing existing ones to enhance the model's predictive behavior

Figure 2.7   Jupyter Notebook environment running on local PC or laptop.

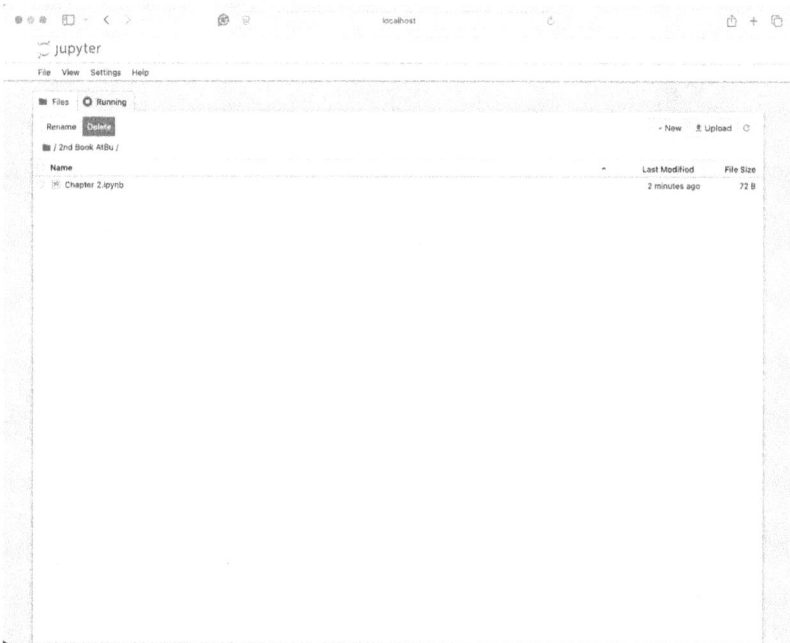

Figure 2.8   Jupyter Notebook environment overview.

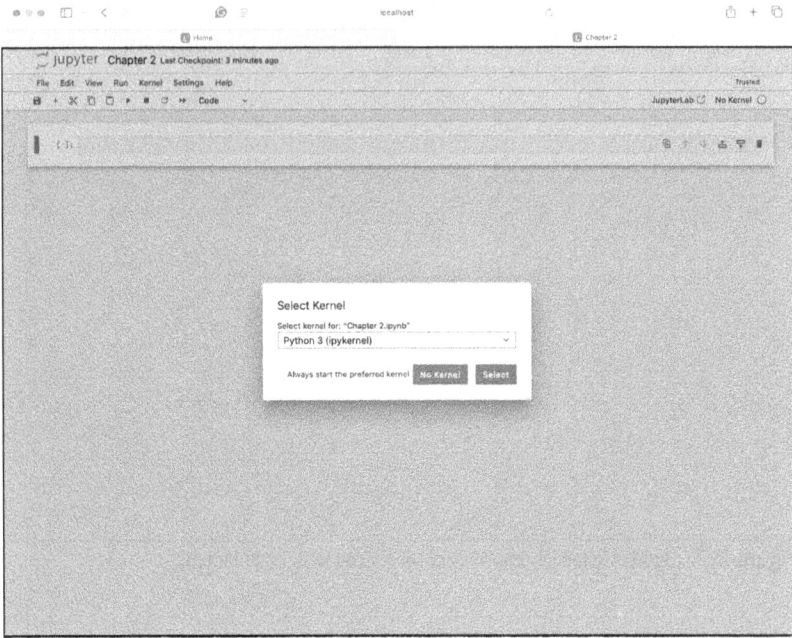

Figure 2.9   Jupyter Notebook with Python programming languages running on local PC or laptop.

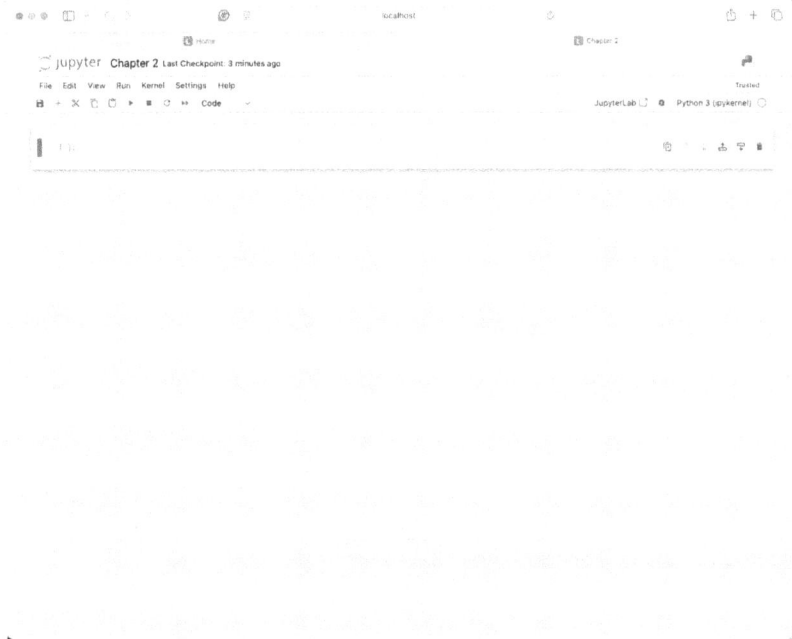

Figure 2.10   Jupyter Notebook environment introduction.

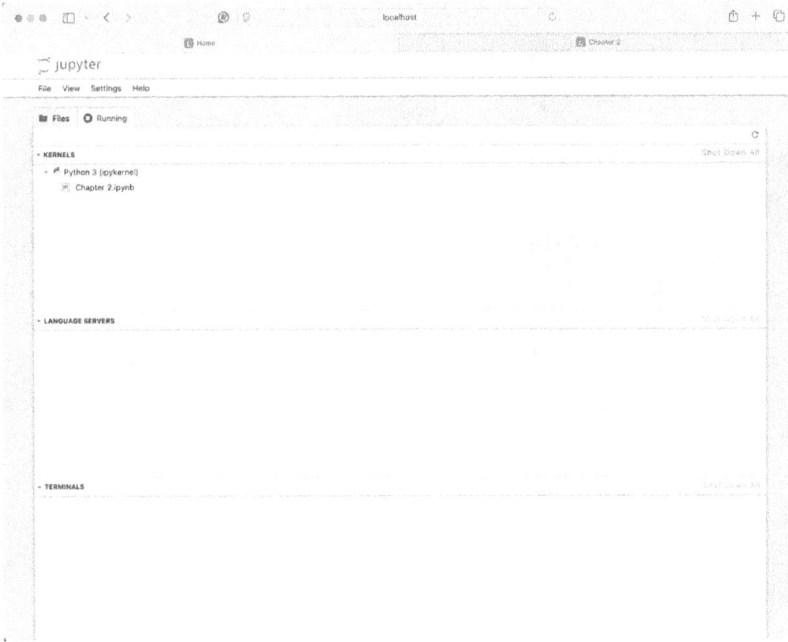

Figure 2.11 Jupyter Notebook environment behind processes with Python programming languages running on local PC or laptop.

performance. This step impacts the model's accuracy and effectiveness. We utilize techniques including normalization, transformation, and adjustment to advance data representativeness power. Now, when we have well-defined features, we move forward with model development. This includes a series of training models utilizing various algorithms and tuning to optimize performance. Cross-validation techniques are used so that the model generalizes well to unseen data and avoids overfitting.

Throughout the model design activity, we highlight clarity and transparency. We attempt to build models that not only behave well but also offer significant insights into the foundational data structures and relationships. This includes choosing models that provide a balance between complexity and clarity, including decision trees, ensemble methods, and neural networks. At last, we meticulously evaluate our models using different performance metrics guided by the related objectives of the project. The metrics used are accuracy, precision, recall, F1-score, ROC-AUC, and others. Based on the evaluation outcome, we repeat the model design, making needed adjustments and advancements to achieve the objectives.

2.2.6   Model Development

Model development activity follows the design steps in the data science lifecycle. This activity includes building and training the models on the previously prepared dataset. We initiate by splitting the dataset into two sets—training and testing sets—to evaluate the model's performance based on the metrics. Different algorithms and techniques are tested in this activity, including three learning techniques—supervised and unsupervised learning and reinforcement learning—based on the available data and the nature of the problem we are addressing. As we stated in the previous section, feature engineering plays a remarkable role in this activity, as it includes generating new features or changing existing ones to advance the model's performance.

Techniques of normalization, scaling, and encoding categorical variables are used to make sure that the dataset is in the best possible shape for training. After the dataset is prepared and features are engineered, we further conduct training on the model. As soon as the model development is concluded and the models meet the performance basis, we move to a production deployment activity.

2.2.7   Model Deployment

Model deployment is related to the activity where a built machine learning (ML) model is implemented into a production environment where its applicability is used to make real-time predictions or lead decision-making processes. This is a key activity in the data science lifecycle as it transforms theoretical models into practical benefits for the industry. The deployment begins with ensuring that the built model is strong and extensible enough to handle real-world data. This includes carrying out vast amounts of testing to validate its behavior and performance under various conditions. Furthermore, the model must be implemented with the actual systems and technology stack, which could involve coding, API development, and adjustment of database configuration to store the prediction data. One of the vital challenges is to maintain and monitor model performance; if that degrades, it is important to have a plan for retraining or retuning with new data. Moreover, deployment activity needs to consider security and compliance; see to it that the model works within the regulatory guidelines and that the data utilized are secured. This could include implementing security controls like encryption, access controls, and regular audits. Generally, model deployment is a continued process that needs maintenance to ensure the model remains effective and relevant during its lifecycle.

2.3   How to Run Predictive Analysis

2.3.1   Steps Involved in Predictive Analysis

In a series of steps included in the predictive analysis, we introduce the following:

- Define the problem, research questions, and analysis types
- Structure the goal
- Select patterns to analyze
- Draw up the problem question
- Define the predictive model structure
- Summarize the findings
- Answer review questions

We will explore in detail and discuss in Chapter 3 all the steps involved in the predictive analysis process.

2.4   Define the Problem, Research Questions, Analysis Types, and Features

Defining the problem includes unearthing the main issue that needs to be fixed, which structures the foundation of the research. Research questions are then expressed to lead the investigation, with a focus on related directions that need to be explored so we can understand the problem. The analysis types are chosen based on the data available and the research question, utilizing methods such as qualitative, quantitative, or mixed-methods analysis to acquire meaningful insights. Features are identified and defined to be integrated into the analysis, ensuring they are related to and relevant to the problem and the general research objectives.

2.5 Structure the Goal

2.5.1 Select Pattern

The selection of the patterns includes selecting a fit mode or methods that are in line with the research objectives and the type of available data. This step is vital as it provides the framework for how the analysis and interpretation of the data are done, which impacts the findings and outcomes of the research.

2.5.2 Problem Question

The problem question is a sensitive part of the construction of the research goals, as it outlines exactly what the research focuses on addressing. Clear, concise, and focused are the standards to be followed, which serves as guidance over the investigation. By identifying the real issue, the problem question makes sure that all the following research activities are in line with solving the main challenges.

2.5.3 Define Predictive Model Structure

Defining the predictive model structure includes drafting the architecture and elements of the model to be utilized in predicting future results based on historical data. This step needs the choice of related algorithms, the foundation of data processing techniques, and the identification of important variables that impact the predictions. By cautiously composing the predictive model, researchers make sure that the model is strong, accurate, and able to provide insightful outcomes that are in line with the research objectives.

2.6 Summary

This chapter discusses the research process, beginning with defining the problem, drafting research questions, and choosing suitable analysis types and features. It talks about defining goals, choosing research patterns, and drafting a clear problem question. Additionally, it defines the predictive model structure, covering selecting algorithms and identifying key variables to ensure accurate predictions.

2.7   Key Terms

- Goal Structure
- Pattern Selection
- Problem Question
- Predictive Model Structure
- Algorithms
- Data Processing Techniques
- Important Variables
- Research Objectives
- Analysis and Interpretation
- Historical Data

2.8   Review Questions

1. What is the first step in the pattern selection process?
+ and defining the problem question.

2. What is essential for creating a predictive model?
A well-defined model structure.

3. Which component is crucial for determining the accuracy of a predictive model?
The choice of algorithms used.

4. How can data be prepared for analysis?
Using various data processing techniques.

5. What helps in identifying the key drivers of the model?
Recognizing important variables.

6. What outlines the goals of the research?
Clearly stated research objectives.

7. How should the findings of a predictive model be communicated?
Through thorough analysis and interpretation.

8. What type of data is reviewed to understand past trends?
Historical data.

9. What ensures the research stays focused and relevant?
Regularly reviewing questions related to the study.

10. What is the final point before moving to external resources?
Addressing the review questions.

11. What might one look for after formulating the review questions?
Suggested websites for additional information.

2.9 Suggested Websites

- Kaggle — [www.kaggle.com]: Data science and machine learning platform.
- Towards Data Science – [https://towardsdatascience.com]: A Medium publication sharing concepts, ideas, and codes.
- DataCamp – [www.datacamp.com]: Enables learning data science online.
- IIoT-WSN-CyberThreat-Dataset – [https://github.com/atdhebuja/IIoT-WSN-CyberThreat-Dataset].

3

DATA ANALYTICS

3.1 Data Analytics

In the evolving field of cybersecurity, data analytics plays a vital role in predicting and mitigating potential threats and risks. By methodically assessing big datasets, we can reveal patterns and insights that are vital for proactive defense approaches. To correctly run data analytics for predictive cybersecurity, various key steps must be taken. Thes include preparing the work environment, defining the methodology and tools used, conducting research scientifically, and utilizing proper tools and Python libraries. Also, data preprocessing, selecting the correct type of analysis, data visualization, and data interpretation are all important elements of the whole process. Integrated, these steps ensure a thorough approach to expecting and addressing cybersecurity issues.

3.2 How to Run Data Analytics for Predictive Cybersecurity

In order to effectively conduct data analytics to advance cybersecurity, it is vital to follow the structured process. This approach starts by preparing the work environment and making sure all needed tools, systems, and personnel are available. After the phase is set, the following step is to define the methodology and tools that will be used throughout the research project. This includes agreeing to scientific research methods to ensure the integrity and reliability of the findings. The options of tools and Python libraries have a notable role in the carrying out of data analytics. Choosing the right tools, as well as consolidating the workflow, also advances the accuracy of the analytics.

DOI: 10.1201/9781003631514-3

Data preprocessing is a distinct critical step; it includes cleaning and organizing the datasets by eliminating any data inconsistencies or errors. Selecting a suitable type of analysis rests on the related objectives of the cybersecurity project. Even if it includes statistical analysis, machine learning, and other techniques, the selection must be in line with the goals of the research. Data visualization is important for interpreting the results and communicating the findings in a very clear way. Further, it supports the identification of trends, patterns, and anomalies that may introduce potential security threats and risks. Finally, by adhering to these thorough steps, organizations can embrace a proactive approach to identifying and mitigating cybersecurity threats.

3.3 Prepare the Environment of Work

The very initial step in preparing the environment of work for data analytics in predictive cybersecurity includes ensuring that all needed tools and systems are properly set up. This would include setting up local or cloud-based environments such as Google Colaboratory or Jupyter Notebook. These platforms are very friendly, use a graphical interface, and support the Python scripting language, which is a vital programming language in the field of data analytics. Google Colaboratory (Colab) provides the utilization of cloud-based execution, where users do not need to install any other third-party software on their local machines, PC, or laptops. The benefits of this option include a shared environment of work with other members and partners and the use of already-installed Python libraries that are utilized in data analytics and machine learning.

On the other hand, Jupyter Notebook, which is going to be installed locally, can be used through the platform Anaconda, which offers a dynamic environment for data analysis. It provides live code execution and visualization of data, and it is easier to test and adjust scripts on the move. Jupyter's large library support offers users the ability to integrate tools such as pandas for data manipulation, matplotlib and seaborn for data visualization and scikit-learn, and TensorFlow for machine learning applications.

Setting up these work environments includes a few vital steps:

1. Google Colaboratory:

- Sign in to a Google account and access Google Colaboratory through the Google Drive interface (Figure 3.1).

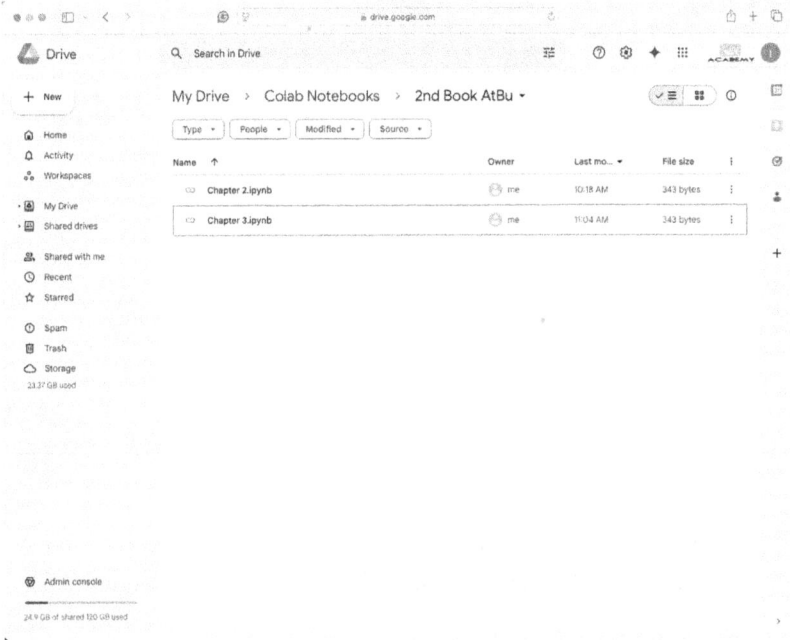

Figure 3.1   Google Colaboratory overview.

- Initiate a new notebook and choose a runtime that includes the necessary computing power (Figure 3.2).

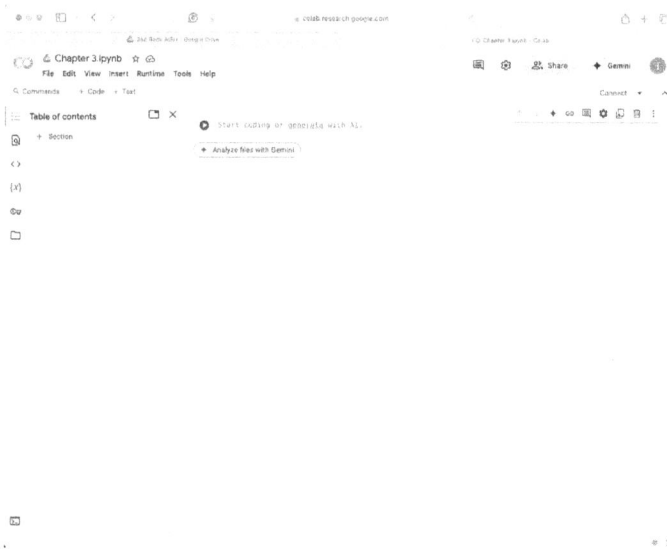

Figure 3.2 New notebook within the Google Colab.

- Install any additional libraries required for the project using the `pip install` command within the notebook (Figure 3.3).

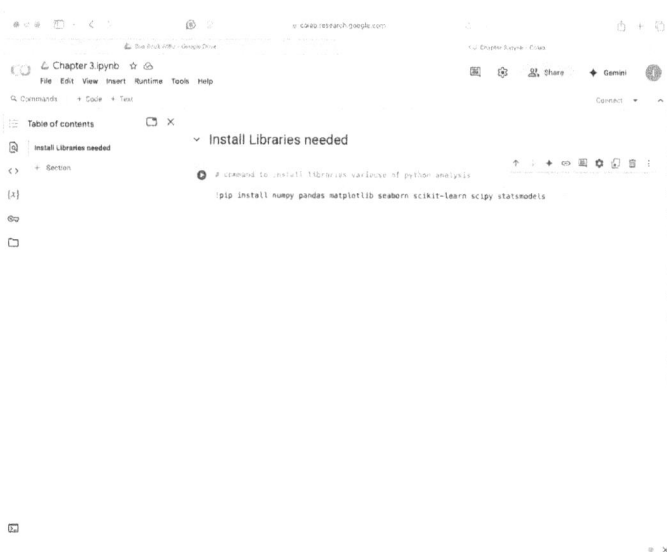

Figure 3.3 Comprehensive view of Python libraries used for data analytics.

2. Jupyter Notebook:

- Install Anaconda, which includes Jupyter Notebook, by downloading the installer from the official website [https://docs.jupyter.org/en/latest/install/notebook-classic.html] and following the installation instructions (Figure 3.4).

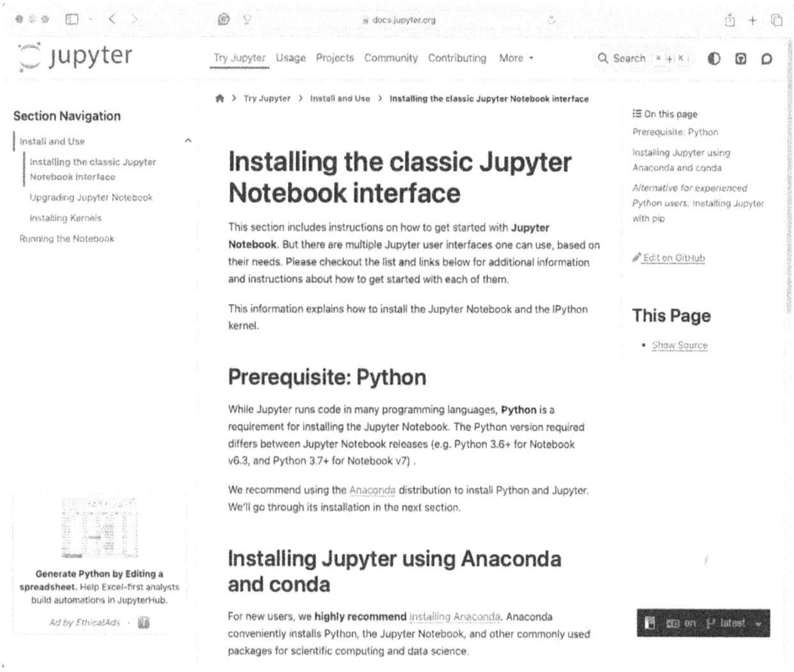

Figure 3.4 Jupyter Notebook installation on local PC or laptop.

- Open Jupyter Notebook from the Anaconda Navigator or by running `jupyter notebook` in the terminal or command prompt (Figure 3.5).

```
                        atdhebuja — -zsh — 80×24
atdhebuja@ABs-Laptop ~ % jupyter notebook
```

Figure 3.5 Launching Jupyter notebook by running 'jupyter notebook' in the terminal.

- Create a new notebook and install any required Python libraries by using the `pip install` command within a cell (Figure 3.6).

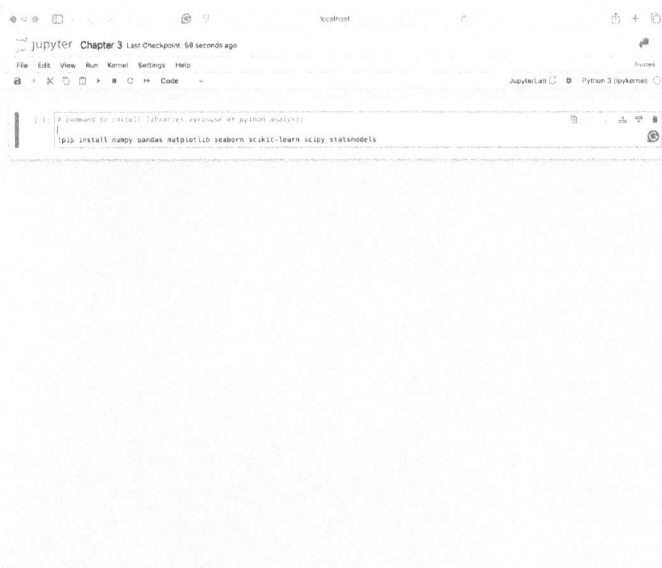

Figure 3.6 New notebook at Jupyter Notebook; install using the 'pip install' command.

By carefully setting up the work environment, consider compatibility with needed tools and libraries and benefit from the powerful capabilities, including Google Colaboratory and Jupyter Notebook. These preparation steps are important for all the following steps and actions of the structured process of the predictive cybersecurity project.

3.4 Specify the Methodology and Tools Utilized

3.4.1 Scientific Research Methods

Scientific research methods are important for engaging in valid studies related to predictive cybersecurity. The methods mentioned include formulating hypotheses, designing experiments, collecting data, and analyzing results. The research process would be reproducible and transparent all the time. The main methodologies cover qualitative and quantitative approaches. Qualitative methods of interviews and case studies offer insights into user behaviors and system vulnerabilities. Quantitative methods offer statistical analyses and mathematical modeling to identify patterns and predict threats. Also, using a combined-methods approach can benefit from the strengths of both qualitative and quantitative techniques, offering a thorough understanding of cybersecurity issues. Essential to this process is the utilization of tools and libraries that support accurate data collection and analysis, including comprehensive documentation to support future research.

3.4.2 Tools and Libraries

Important to the success of predictive cybersecurity projects are the tools and libraries that support the analysis and visualization of data. The most used tools include:

- Python – A versatile programming language that supports a wide variety of libraries tailored for data science and machine learning, making it a staple in cybersecurity research.
- Pandas – An essential library for data manipulation and analysis, offering data structures and operations for manipulating numerical tables and time series.
- NumPy – Fundamental for scientific computing with Python, providing support for arrays, matrices, and a multitude of mathematical functions.

- Scikit-learn – A robust library for machine learning that includes simple and efficient tools for data mining and data analysis.
- Matplotlib and Seaborn – Libraries for creating static, animated, and interactive visualizations in Python, crucial for data visualization and interpretation.
- TensorFlow and PyTorch – Popular deep learning frameworks that support the development and training of complex neural network models.
- Jupyter Notebook – An open-source web application that allows the creation and sharing of documents containing live code, equations, visualizations, and narrative text.
- Google Colaboratory – A free, cloud-based tool that provides a Jupyter Notebook environment, enabling the use of powerful computing resources for research.

3.5   Data Preprocessing

Data preprocessing is a key step in the analysis series, focused on transforming raw data into a clean and ready-to-use format for further processing in the data science lifecycle. The process includes some phases:

1. Data Cleaning: This stage focuses on identifying and correcting errors or inconsistencies in the data, such as missing or duplicated values, outliers, and incorrect data entries. Techniques like imputation, interpolation, and outlier detection are commonly employed.
2. Data Integration: Combining data from multiple sources to create a unified dataset. This step may involve data warehousing, data merging, and the resolution of data format differences.
3. Data Transformation: Converting data into a suitable format for analysis. This can include normalization or scaling of features, encoding categorical variables, and applying mathematical transformations to enhance data interpretability.
4. Data Reduction: Simplifying the data by reducing its dimensionality, which helps in improving processing time and model performance. Techniques such as principal component analysis (PCA) and feature selection are commonly used.

5. Data Discretization: This involves converting continuous data into discrete buckets or intervals, often necessary for specific types of analysis or certain machine learning models.

Successful data preprocessing stands as the base for accurate and insightful analysis, making sure that the coming steps in the project cycle, including model training and evaluation, can be utilized proficiently.

3.6   Analysis Type Selection

Choosing a suitable type of analysis is vital for extracting useful insights from the data. This selection depends mainly on the research question, data characteristics, and the desired results of the study. There are various types of analysis, including descriptive analysis, exploratory analysis, inferential analysis, predictive analysis, prescriptive analysis, and causal analysis. In the common types of analyses listed below, we will elaborate on and introduce the importance of data analytics for predictive cybersecurity.

- Descriptive Analysis: Provides a summary of the data's main features using measures of mean, median, and standard deviation, as well as visualizations such as histograms and box plots.
- Exploratory Data Analysis (EDA): Involves investigating the data to discover patterns, anomalies, or relationships. Techniques such as clustering and correlation analysis can be used to uncover hidden structures. This analysis is introduced in detail in Chapter 4, which we will use throughout this book for predictive cybersecurity.
- Inferential Analysis: Utilizes statistical tests to make inferences about the population based on sample data. This includes hypothesis testing, confidence intervals, and regression analysis.
- Predictive Analysis: Focuses on building models to predict future outcomes based on historical data. Techniques include linear regression, decision trees, and machine learning algorithms.

- Prescriptive Analysis: Provides recommendations for decision-making by considering different scenarios and their potential impacts. Optimization and simulation models are often employed in this type.
- Causal Analysis: Aims to understand cause-and-effect relationships within the data. Methods such as randomized controlled trials and instrumental variable analysis are commonly used.

After the analysis type is selected, the following steps include data visualization.

3.7   Data Visualization

Data visualization plays a crucial role in the analysis process by changing complex datasets into a thorough visual presentation. Constructive visualization makes sure researchers and decision-makers instantly take note of the foundational trends, patterns, and outliers in the data. Different tools and techniques can be used to generate convincing visual representations (charts, graphs, and maps). Visualizations such as bar charts, pie charts, and line graphs are commonly used for illustrating relationships and comparisons within the data. More enhanced visualizations, like heat maps and network diagrams, can reveal deeper insights by highlighting connections and densities. The choice of visualization depends on the specific analysis goals and the nature of the data. Tools such as Tableau and Power BI, and Python libraries like Matplotlib and Seaborn, are widely used for creating high-quality visualizations.

3.8   Data Interpretation

Data interpretation includes an understanding of the visualized data outcome, meaningful insights, and conclusions that can inform the decision-making process. It is the step where statistical and analytical findings are translated into practical, actionable recommendations. During this phase, analysts examine the visual representations to identify patterns, trends, correlations, and anomalies and relate them to the research questions or business problems. Effective data interpretation requires a combination of domain knowledge, critical thinking, and statistical expertise. The ultimate goal of data interpretation is to transform raw data into a coherent narrative that provides clarity and direction. This narrative should highlight key findings, explain their significance, and propose recommendations for action.

3.9 Summary

This chapter discusses the significance of various analytical methods, the importance of data visualization, and the interpretation process. By following these steps, one can derive meaningful insights from raw data and make informed decisions. The chapter also underlines the role of advanced visualization tools and the necessity of domain knowledge for effective data interpretation.

3.10 Key Terms

- Prescriptive Analysis
- Optimization and Simulation Models
- Causal Analysis
- Randomized Controlled Trials
- Instrumental Variable Analysis
- Data Visualization
- Bar Charts
- Pie Charts
- Line Graphs
- Heat Maps
- Network Diagrams
- Tableau
- Power BI
- Matplotlib
- Seaborn
- Data Interpretation
- Domain Knowledge
- Critical Thinking
- Statistical Expertise

3.11   Review Questions

1. What is the primary purpose of Network Diagrams in data analysis?
Network Diagrams are used to visualize relationships and flows between nodes, such as in social networks or communication networks, making it easier to understand complex connections.

2. How can Tableau be used in data visualization?
Tableau is a powerful tool for creating interactive and shareable dashboards that present data in a visually appealing format, helping to uncover insights and trends.

3. What distinguishes Power BI from other data visualization tools?
Power BI integrates seamlessly with Microsoft products, offers robust data connectivity options, and provides advanced analytics and visualization capabilities for business intelligence purposes.

4. Explain the difference between Matplotlib and Seaborn.
Matplotlib is a versatile plotting library in Python that allows for detailed customization, while Seaborn is built on top of Matplotlib and simplifies the creation of attractive and informative statistical graphics.

5. Why is Data Interpretation crucial in data analysis?
Data Interpretation involves making sense of numerical data by identifying patterns, trends, and relationships, which is essential for informed decision-making and drawing accurate conclusions.

6. How does Domain Knowledge enhance data analysis?
Domain Knowledge provides the context and understanding necessary to interpret data correctly, identify relevant variables, and produce meaningful and actionable insights specific to a particular field or industry.

7. What role does Critical Thinking play in data analysis?
Critical Thinking involves evaluating data logically and systematically, questioning assumptions, and making reasoned judgments, which is vital for uncovering hidden insights and solving complex problems.

8. Describe the importance of Statistical Expertise in data analysis.

Statistical Expertise equips analysts with the skills to apply appropriate statistical methods, interpret results accurately, and ensure the validity and reliability of findings, thereby enhancing the overall quality of analysis.

9. What is the significance of Review Questions in a learning module?

Review Questions reinforce key concepts, assess comprehension, and help learners identify areas of strength and areas in need of improvement, facilitating better retention and understanding of the material.

10. How can one effectively use Suggested Websites for further learning?

Suggested Websites can provide additional resources, tutorials, and real-world examples that complement the learning material, offering diverse perspectives and deeper insights into the subject matter.

11. What are some best practices for creating effective Data Visualizations?

Best practices include choosing the right type of visualization for the data, maintaining simplicity and clarity, using colors and labels effectively, and ensuring that the visualization tells a coherent and impactful story.

3.12   Suggested Websites

- Kaggle – [www.kaggle.com]: Data science and machine learning platform.
- Towards Data Science – [https://towardsdatascience.com]: A Medium publication sharing concepts, ideas, and codes.
- DataCamp – [www.datacamp.com]: Enables learning data science online.
- The Jupyter project – [https://jupyter.org].
- Google Colab – [https://colab.google].

4

EXPLORATORY DATA ANALYSIS (EDA) FOR CYBERSECURITY INSIGHTS

4.1 Exploratory Data Analysis for Cybersecurity Insights

In this chapter, we deep-dive into the process of exploratory data analysis (EDA) guided for cybersecurity applications. EDA is a key step in understanding the data and highlighting patterns and anomalies in cybersecurity datasets that can expose insights important for advancing protection mechanisms. Based on the guidance data science lifecycle roadmap introduced in Chapter 2, EDA represents a very crucial question: how are variables related?

EDA includes various steps from data collection and preprocessing, ensuring data is clean and ready for analysis (Figure 4.1). The next step is data visualization, where different visualizations (histograms, scatter plots, and box plots) support identifying trends and patterns. Tools like Python's Pandas, Matplotlib, and Seaborn are commonly used for this analysis. Consequent visualization and statistical analysis are performed to quantify relationships and test hypotheses. Descriptive statistics (mean, median, standard deviation, and variance) offer a summary of the data's central tendency and dispersion. Inferential statistics (regression analysis and hypothesis testing) provide guidance in making predictions and drawing conclusions from the data. A distinct key aspect of EDA in cybersecurity is anomaly detection, pattern recognition, etc.

During the exploration phase for a proper design step of EDA, we list potential scenarios or ideas, problem definitions, or research

DOI: 10.1201/9781003631514-4

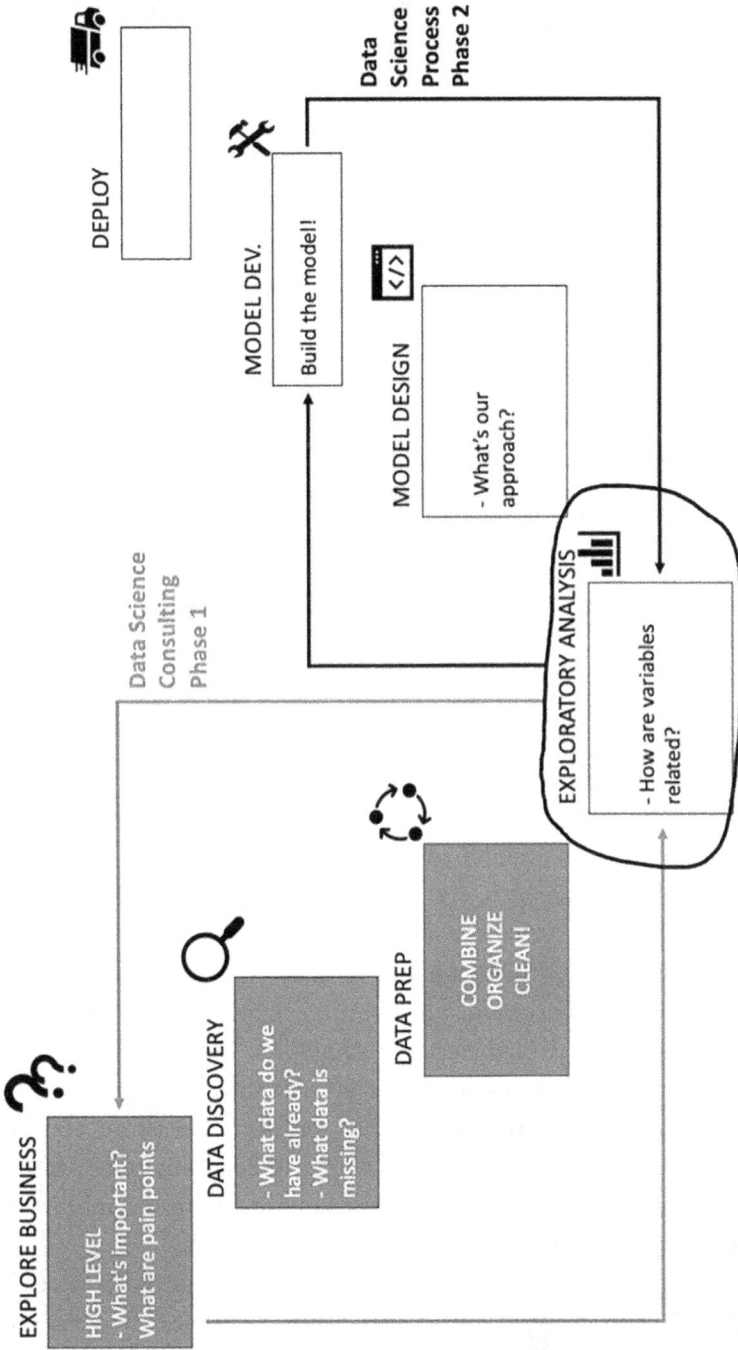

Figure 4.1 Data science lifecycle roadmap.

Table 4.1 Example of EDA Analysis Type

SCENARIO/ IDEA	PROBLEM/ RESEARCH QUESTION	ANALYSIS TYPE
1. Attack Trend Analysis	What are the trends in attack occurrences over time?	Time-Series Analysis
2. Geo IP Analysis	Can we identify geographical sources of attacks?	Geospatial Analysis
3. Attack Tactics Identification	What are the common attack tactics used by attackers?	Pattern Recognition
4. Anomaly Detection	Can we identify unusual attack patterns?	Anomaly Detection
5. Attack Vector Prediction	Can we predict potential attack vectors?	Classification or Forecasting
6. Industry Sector Vulnerability Assessment	Which industry sectors are frequently targeted?	Clustering or Classification
7. Attack Origin Trends	How are attack origins changing over time?	Time-Series Analysis
8. Geo IP Pattern Analysis	Are there specific attack patterns based on location?	Pattern Recognition, Geospatial Analysis
9. Attacker Behavior Clustering	Can we group attackers based on behavior?	Clustering
10. Impact Assessment on Industry Sectors	Which industry sector is most impacted by attacks?	Impact Analysis
11. Attack Timeline Sequencing	What is the sequence of actions in an attack?	Sequence Analysis
12. Predictive Maintenance of Attacks	Can we predict potential future attack trends?	Time-Series Forecasting

questions related to predictive cybersecurity. Table 4.1 introduces potential types of analysis for our predictive cybersecurity project. So, we'll relate the scenario to the appropriate analysis type, where a problem or research question will be answered from the result of a certain analysis conducted. Further, in Chapter 5, we will include feature selection and engineering techniques. These scenarios pose questions related to predicting future attack trends, identifying likely attack vectors, anticipating vulnerable sensors, forecasting attacker behaviors, and detecting anomalies that may indicate emerging attacks. It's important to note that some scenarios might require a combination of analysis techniques to gain comprehensive insights.

Over a series of structured steps, we will examine how to select the related analysis type, define and refine our research questions, and conduct EDA techniques to draw meaningful conclusions. This direction will lead to predictive cybersecurity projects, but also to the identification of threats and vulnerabilities. In the following section, we will start with the selection of the appropriate type of analysis for our dataset.

4.2   Analysis Type Selection

Once the analysis type is chosen, the next step is to define the research question. Since our cybersecurity project is predictive, we focus on the selected analysis type that follows the nature of the project. After business exploration, data discovery, and understanding, a predictive analysis type is selected as having the potential to provide better results and guide us in this research work. A precise research question is important as it guides the whole EDA process and supports the determination of the related methods and tools to use.

4.3   Define the Research Question

A clearly defined research question is vital as it leads the whole analysis and supports the examination of Indicators of Compromise (IoC) based on the data. A question related to our predictive cybersecurity project research could be: "Can we develop a predictive model that identifies potential IIoT and WSN attacks in advance and recommends countermeasures to mitigate the attacks effectively?" This question directs our analysis toward predictive maintenance that predicts attacks and takes countermeasures in advance. The goal is to create a model that can predict potential attacks before they occur and provide actionable insights to prevent or mitigate these attacks. Once the research question is defined, the following step is the running EDA analysis (data collection and preprocessing phase). Relevant datasets could include logs, network traffic, and incident reports. With the insights from EDA analysis, we can refine our research question further if necessary and proceed to developing predictive models.

4.4   How to Answer the Research Question

A way of answering the defined research question includes a structured approach to make sure that the analysis is thorough and stands. Based on the defined scope and objectives of the research project, we try to answer the question. This includes understanding first the related IoC of the cyberattacks we are focused on and how they manifest within the dataset based on selection analysis. Ensuring data quality at this moment is vital to avoid biases and inaccuracies that could affect the analysis outcome. EDA is an iterative process that includes summarizing the characteristics of the data and presenting them from an understanding viewpoint. Visualizations (histograms, scatter plots, and heatmaps) are important tools for identifying patterns, trends, and anomalies in the data.

4.5 How to Run EDA for Predictive Cybersecurity

To run EDA for predictive cybersecurity, we start by having the dataset in place. Once that is prepared and ready, we move to conducting the exploratory data analysis (EDA) based on the analysis type we choose from the above table, scenario, or idea. In the following part of this section, we will conduct hands-on research and run prepared Python scripting, which will guide us through the iterative EDA process of summarizing the main characteristics of the dataset. Over this stage, we use various statistical tools and visualizations to uncover patterns, trends, and anomalies. By utilizing these EDA techniques, we will have a deeper understanding of the data and structure. This understanding is vital; through identifying key indicators and variables that impact potential attacks, we can refine our research question if necessary. Based on the scenarios for EDA presented in Table 4.1, we will select two scenarios for analysis.

I. First, the selected EDA scenario will be Attack Trend analysis, followed by the defined research question: "What are the trends in attack occurrences over time?" The analysis type conducted will be Time-series, focusing on two tasks: analyzing attack frequency over time and detecting seasonal patterns in cyberthreats.

II. Second, the selected EDA scenario will be Geo IP analysis, followed by the defined research question: "Can we identify the geographical sources of attacks?" The analysis type conducted will be Geospatial, focusing on two tasks: visualizing attack sources on a world map and identifying high-risk regions for IIoT/WSN cyberthreats.

For our project, we will utilize an example dataset named "**IIoT-WSN_CyberThreats**" with sample data to demonstrate the entire data science lifecycle process of predictive cybersecurity in the Industrial Internet of Things (IIoT) and wireless sensor networks (WSNs).

I. Attack Trend Analysis

The process begins by running an EDA analysis Attack Trend further along the following steps. For each step, a series of custom Python scripts will be written and will be presented in the figures with the results in the next section (Section 4.6 or Section 4.7) and the Data Interpretation section (Section 4.8).

Step 1: Overview of the dataset (which will be uploaded on Google Drive), using the Google Colab environment. A Python script pandas library has been used to read the dataset named "**IIoT-WSN_CyberThreats**" and display the first few rows of the dataset. Here is the main script that generates the overview of the dataset:

```python
# Here is the Python script you can run in
Google Colab to read and display the first
few rows of # the "IIoT-WSN_CyberThreats"
dataset using the pandas library.

# Import necessary libraries
import pandas as pd

# Define dataset path (ensure the file is
uploaded to Google Drive)
dataset_path = "/content/drive/MyDrive/
Colab Notebooks/2nd Book AtBu/IIoT-WSN_
CyberThreats.csv"

# Read the dataset
df = pd.read_csv(dataset_path)
# Display the first few rows
```

```
print("First five rows of the dataset:")
display(df.head())
# Get total number of rows and columns

num_rows, num_columns = df.shape
print(f"\nTotal Rows: {num_rows}")
print(f"Total Columns: {num_columns}")

# Display dataset information
print("\nDataset Information:")
df.info()
```

Step 2: The data.describe() method is used to generate summary statistics of the numerical columns. It provides a quick overview of the central tendencies and spread of the data. Here is the script:

```
# Import necessary libraries
import pandas as pd

# Define dataset path (ensure the file is
uploaded to Google Drive)
dataset_path = "/content/drive/MyDrive/
Colab Notebooks/2nd Book AtBu/IIoT-WSN_
CyberThreats.csv"

# Read the dataset
df = pd.read_csv(dataset_path)

# Display summary statistics of numerical
columns
print("\nSummary Statistics of Numerical
Columns:")
display(df.describe())
```

Step 3: Now that we have explored the dataset using various methods in the previous steps, we need to perform exploratory data analysis (EDA) specific to our research questions. The next script will engage EDA tasks, including converting the timestamp column to datetime format, grouping & aggregating attack counts over time, plotting time-series trends, and identifying attack type trends. Run the following script in Google Colab to start analyzing attack trends over time:

```
# Import necessary libraries
import pandas as pd
import matplotlib.pyplot as plt

# Define dataset path
dataset_path = "/content/drive/MyDrive/
Colab Notebooks/2nd Book AtBu/IIoT-WSN_
CyberThreats.csv"

# Read dataset
df = pd.read_csv(dataset_path)

# Convert Timestamp column to datetime
format
df["Timestamp"] = pd.to_
datetime(df["Timestamp"])

# Set Timestamp as index
df.set_index("Timestamp", inplace=True)
# Resample data to get daily attack counts
attack_trend = df[df["Malicious_Activity"]
== 1].resample("D").size()

# Plot attack trend over time
plt.figure(figsize=(12,6))
plt.plot(attack_trend, marker='o',
linestyle='-', label="Daily Attack Count")
plt.xlabel("Date")
plt.ylabel("Number of Attacks")
plt.title("Attack Trend Over Time")
plt.legend()
plt.grid(True)
plt.show()
```

Step 4: We will further analyze trends so that we will be able to smooth variations and identify meaningful patterns. Here is the script that smooths out variations and detects anomalies in attack trends using a rolling average and anomaly detection.

```
# Apply a Rolling Average to Identify
Trends
import pandas as pd
import matplotlib.pyplot as plt

# Define dataset path
dataset_path = "/content/drive/MyDrive/
Colab Notebooks/2nd Book AtBu/IIoT-WSN_
CyberThreats.csv"

# Read dataset
df = pd.read_csv(dataset_path)

# Convert Timestamp column to datetime
format
df["Timestamp"] = pd.to_
datetime(df["Timestamp"])

# Set Timestamp as index
df.set_index("Timestamp", inplace=True)

# Resample data to get daily attack counts
attack_trend = df[df["Malicious_Activity"]
== 1].resample("D").size()

# Apply a rolling average with a 7-day
window
rolling_avg = attack_trend.rolling(window=
7).mean()

# Plot original attack trend vs rolling
average
plt.figure(figsize=(12,6))
```

```
plt.plot(attack_trend, marker='o',
linestyle='-', alpha=0.5, label="Daily
Attack Count")
plt.plot(rolling_avg, color='red',
linewidth=2, label="7-Day Rolling
Average")
plt.xlabel("Date")
plt.ylabel("Number of Attacks")
plt.title("Attack Trend with 7-Day Rolling
Average")
plt.legend()
plt.grid(True)
plt.show()

# Apply Anomaly Detection
import numpy as np

# Compute Interquartile Range (IQR) for
anomaly detection
Q1 = attack_trend.quantile(0.25)
Q3 = attack_trend.quantile(0.75)
IQR = Q3 - Q1

# Define attack anomalies (beyond 1.5 * IQR
range)
anomaly_threshold_high = Q3 + 1.5 * IQR
anomalies = attack_trend[attack_trend >
anomaly_threshold_high]

# Plot attack trend with anomalies highlighted
plt.figure(figsize=(12,6))
plt.plot(attack_trend, marker='o',
linestyle='-', alpha=0.5, label="Daily
Attack Count")
plt.scatter(anomalies.index, anomalies,
color='red', label="Detected Anomalies",
zorder=3)
plt.xlabel("Date")
```

```
plt.ylabel("Number of Attacks")
plt.title("Anomaly Detection in Attack
Trends")
plt.legend()
plt.grid(True)
plt.show()
```

II. Geo IP Analysis

The process begins by running an EDA analysis Geo IP further along the following steps. For each step, a series of custom Python scripts will be written and will be presented in the figures with the results in the next section (Section 4.6 or Section 4.7) and the Data Interpretation section (Section 4.8).

Step 1: We will load the dataset, extract attack-related records (Malicious_Activity == 1), and extract latitude and longitude from the geolocation field. Here is the script for it:

```
# Load the dataset
# Extract attack-related records
(Malicious_Activity == 1)
# Extract latitude and longitude from the
Geo_Location field

import pandas as pd
import ast

# Define dataset path
dataset_path = "/content/drive/MyDrive/
Colab Notebooks/2nd Book AtBu/IIoT-WSN_
CyberThreats.csv"

# Read dataset
df = pd.read_csv(dataset_path)

# Convert Timestamp column to datetime format
df["Timestamp"] = pd.to_
datetime(df["Timestamp"])
```

```
# Extract attacks only
df_attacks = df[df["Malicious_Activity"] =
= 1].copy()

# Extract latitude and longitude from Geo_
Location
df_attacks["Latitude"] = df_attacks["Geo_
Location"].apply(lambda x: ast.literal_
eval(x)[0])
df_attacks["Longitude"] = df_attacks["Geo_
Location"].apply(lambda x: ast.literal_
eval(x)[1])

# Display the first few rows
print("First few attack records with
geographical information:")
display(df_attacks[["Source_IP",
"Latitude", "Longitude", "Attack_Type"]].
head())
```

Step 2: We are looking to find high-risk regions. With the next script, we count the number of attacks per location.

```
# To find high-risk regions, we count the
number of attacks per location.

# Count attacks by location (Latitude,
Longitude)
attack_counts = df_attacks.
groupby(["Latitude", "Longitude"]).size().
reset_index(name="Attack_Count")

# Display the top 10 high-risk regions
print("Top 10 High-Risk Regions:")
display(attack_counts.sort_values(by=
"Attack_Count", ascending=False).head(10))
```

Step 3: In this script, we will use Folium and HeatMap to create a density visualization.

```
# We will use Folium + HeatMap to create a
density visualization.

from folium.plugins import HeatMap

# Create a new map
heatmap = folium.Map(location=[df_
attacks["Latitude"].mean(), df_
attacks["Longitude"].mean()], zoom_start=
2)

# Add heatmap layer
HeatMap(data=df_attacks[["Latitude",
"Longitude"]].values, radius=10).add_
to(heatmap)

# Save the heatmap file
heatmap_path = "GeoIP_Attack_Heatmap.html"
heatmap.save(heatmap_path)

# Download the heatmap file
files.download(heatmap_path)
```

4.6   Generate Results

The results generated from the predictive analysis need to be assessed thoroughly to ensure reliability and effectiveness (Figures 4.2–4.4). Additionally, the evaluation in Chapter 5 will explain testing the models on historical data and new data to validate their predictive power. Key performance metrics such as accuracy, precision, recall, and F1-score are utilized to assess the models' performance.

First five rows of the dataset:

	Timestamp	Device_ID	Device_Type	Protocol	Source_IP	Destination_IP	Geo_Location	Packet_Size	Request_Type	Payload_Entropy	CPU_Usage (%)	Memory_Usage (%)	Temperature (°C)	Battery_Level (%)	Malicious_Activity	Attack_Type
0	2025-01-12 02:09:38.801740	DEV-0	Actuator	CoAP	192.168.66.248	192.168.213.235	(-62.282725, -107.082729)	1176	PUBLISH	4.507267	10.473321	11.055642	-16.488181	44.982328	1	Malware
1	2024-10-07 22:52:38.801740	DEV-1	Gateway	CoAP	192.168.175.24	192.168.231.227	(73.940972, 91.792158)	910	SUBSCRIBE	6.430439	91.543859	35.355775	41.737370	84.735003	1	Brute Force
2	2024-09-22 05:44:38.801740	DEV-2	Gateway	Modbus	192.168.23.50	192.168.198.237	(-20.119692, 152.560421)	1344	PUBLISH	1.097188	10.012595	54.287022	39.644889	30.190023	0	NaN
3	2025-01-30 16:21:38.801740	DEV-3	Sensor	MQTT	192.168.235.8	192.168.186.172	(-62.867782, -142.827208)	1180	POST	4.645593	65.172709	81.317597	15.445638	37.181287	0	NaN
4	2024-11-06 18:05:38.801740	DEV-4	Sensor	Modbus	192.168.63.80	192.168.166.204	(-4.532208, -123.604478)	1145	POST	4.044070	41.906263	22.427865	14.314200	16.482188	0	NaN

```
Total Rows: 5000
Total Columns: 16

Dataset Information:
<class 'pandas.core.frame.DataFrame'>
RangeIndex: 5000 entries, 0 to 4999
Data columns (total 16 columns):
 #   Column             Non-Null Count   Dtype
---  ------             --------------   -----
 0   Timestamp          5000 non-null    object
 1   Device_ID          5000 non-null    object
 2   Device_Type        5000 non-null    object
 3   Protocol           5000 non-null    object
 4   Source_IP          5000 non-null    object
 5   Destination_IP     5000 non-null    object
 6   Geo_Location       5000 non-null    object
 7   Packet_Size        5000 non-null    int64
 8   Request_Type       5000 non-null    object
 9   Payload_Entropy    5000 non-null    float64
 10  CPU_Usage (%)      5000 non-null    float64
 11  Memory_Usage (%)   5000 non-null    float64
 12  Temperature (°C)   5000 non-null    float64
 13  Battery_Level (%)  5000 non-null    float64
 14  Malicious_Activity 5000 non-null    int64
 15  Attack_Type        855 non-null     object
dtypes: float64(5), int64(2), object(9)
memory usage: 625.1+ KB
```

Figure 4.2 Overview of the dataset – total rows, 5000; total columns, 16.

Summary Statistics of Numerical Columns:

	Packet_Size	Payload_Entropy	CPU_Usage (%)	Memory_Usage (%)	Temperature (°C)	Battery_Level (%)	Malicious_Activity
count	5000.000000	5000.000000	5000.000000	5000.000000	5000.000000	5000.000000	5000.00000
mean	782.664000	3.930786	50.383344	50.919986	15.904034	49.283658	0.20040
std	416.252336	2.297878	28.484682	28.498775	20.336092	28.529554	0.40034
min	50.000000	0.000246	1.005230	1.024993	-19.996631	0.011023	0.00000
25%	429.750000	1.938489	25.963954	26.213731	-1.658193	24.852832	0.00000
50%	791.000000	3.873591	50.043454	51.298157	16.212085	49.010695	0.00000
75%	1142.000000	5.906851	75.205588	75.709000	33.444708	73.091180	0.00000
max	1499.000000	7.996462	99.967647	99.992558	49.993068	99.969561	1.00000

Figure 4.3 Summary statistics of the data distribution.

	Source_IP	Latitude	Longitude	Attack_Type
0	192.168.66.248	-62.262725	-107.082729	Malware
1	192.168.175.24	73.940972	91.792158	Brute Force
16	192.168.0.109	45.369136	93.210117	MITM
17	192.168.244.39	51.719000	-152.220974	DDoS
26	192.168.160.188	59.417577	-178.535906	NaN

Figure 4.4 First few attack records with geographical information.

	Latitude	Longitude	Attack_Count
0	-89.529530	111.903842	1
672	29.851960	-31.703494	1
659	27.703711	-81.196421	1
660	28.118745	47.635351	1
661	28.200060	-167.592019	1
662	28.283963	141.039830	1
663	28.362725	54.076641	1
664	28.376644	103.548921	1
665	28.409215	-172.515198	1
666	28.618026	144.360025	1

Figure 4.5 Top 10 high-risk regions.

4.7   Data Visualization

The utilization of data visualization techniques is vital for communicating the findings from the EDA analysis process. Various visualizations (histograms, scatter plots, and heatmaps) can emphasize key patterns, trends, and anomalies within the dataset (Figures 4.6–4.9). These visualizations lead to understanding the data and explaining the findings to stakeholders with consideration of both technical and nontechnical backgrounds.

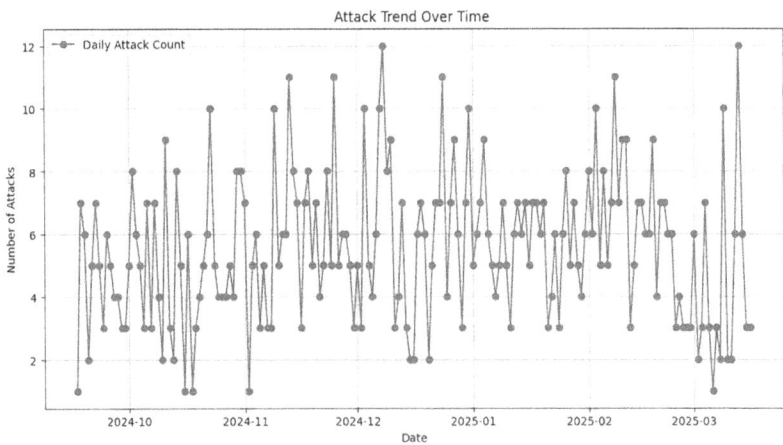

Figure 4.6   Attack trend over time.

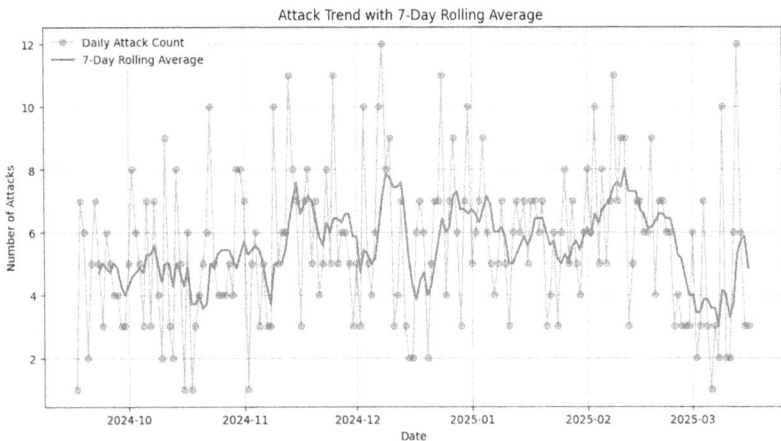

Figure 4.7   Attack trend with 7-day rolling average.

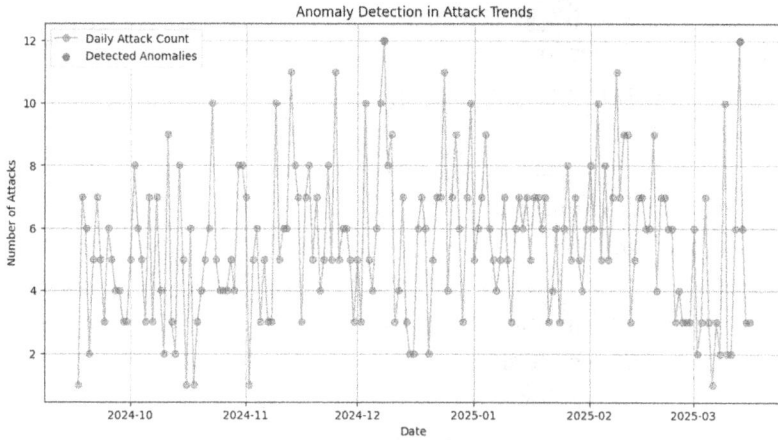

Figure 4.8 Anomaly detection in attack trends.

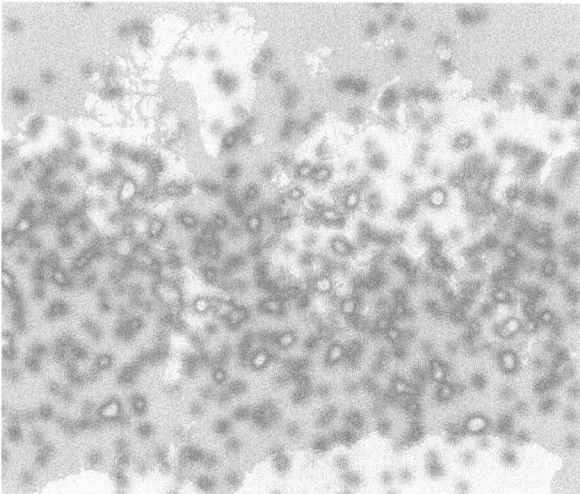

Figure 4.9 Heatmap visualization of the attack regions (sample data used).

4.8 Data Interpretation

Interpretation of the data and results is the final phase in our EDA analysis process. This includes concluding insights from the visualizations and statistical analyses conducted. The interpretation of results is in the context of our predictive cybersecurity goals, translating the findings into actionable strategies that can advance security measures and mitigate potential threats. By understanding the significance of the identified patterns and trends, we can prioritize domains for further investigation and develop robust defenses against cyberattacks. Effective data interpretation closes the gap between data analysis and practical application, making sure that the insights from EDA analysis are leveraged to their fullest potential in creating a secure digital environment.

Figure 4.3 summarizes statistics that indicate that CPU and memory utilization are well distributed (averaging around 50% utilization). Packet sizes vary significantly (ranging from 50 bytes to 1499 bytes). Payload entropy, which measures randomness (has an average of 3.93), suggests some variation in data structure. Around 20% of the data points are labeled as malicious activity, which is sufficient for training a predictive model.

Figure 4.4 visualizes the attack trend over time, which shows variations in the daily attack count over the analyzed period. Key observations include:

- Attack occurrences are highly variable, with spikes reaching up to 12 attacks per day.
- There is no clear increasing or decreasing long-term trend, but periodic surges suggest seasonal attack patterns.
- Some periods experience low attack rates (1–3 per day), while others show frequent high-attack peaks.
- The oscillating nature indicates that attacks may follow specific time patterns, potentially linked to system vulnerabilities or attacker strategies.

Figure 4.7 visualizes the attack trend analysis using a 7-day rolling average surface periodic variations in attack occurrences over time. The red line smooths out daily variations, highlighting seasonal trends where attack frequency increases mid-period and then declines slightly. This means that IIoT and WSN cyberthreats follow recurring patterns, which could be linked to attacker behavior, system vulnerabilities, or external triggers. Identifying these patterns supports predictive modeling and proactive cybersecurity measures.

Figure 4.8 visualizes the anomaly detection and highlights significant attack spikes, marked by red dots, which indicate that unusual attacks occurred. These anomalies may be related to targeted cyberattacks, system misconfigurations, or large-scale threat campaigns. Investigating these anomalies further can help pinpoint root causes and improve defensive strategies. Overall, this analysis partially answers the research question by confirming that attack trends exist, but further investigation into causal factors and forecasting models could provide deeper insights.

The results (Figures 4.4, 4.5, and 4.9) provide a geospatial distribution of attack sources, confirming that attacks originate from various locations across the globe. Figure 4.4 shows attack source IPs along with their geographical locations and attack types, revealing that various attack methods (e.g., Malware, Brute Force, MITM, and DDoS) are associated with different regions. Figure 4.5 highlights high-risk regions where attacks are concentrated, although each location in this dataset has a relatively low count per coordinate. The heatmap visualization in Figure 4.9 further confirms that attacks are widespread, with hotspots appearing in North America, South America, Europe, and Asia, suggesting higher cyberthreat activity in these areas. Yes, we have partially answered the research question.

4.9   Summary

This chapter discusses the importance of the exploratory data analysis (EDA) process, tools, visualization, and the interpretation process. In addition to these technical aspects, it is also vital to consider the ethical implications of data analysis in cybersecurity. Ensuring the privacy and confidentiality of the data is important, and strict protocols must be followed when handling sensitive information.

4.10   Key Terms

- Attack Occurrences
- Seasonal Attack Patterns
- IIoT (Industrial Internet of Things)
- WSNs (Wireless Sensor Networks)
- Cyberthreats
- Predictive Modeling
- Proactive Cybersecurity Measures

- Anomaly Detection
- Targeted Cyberattacks
- System Misconfigurations
- Threat Campaigns
- Geospatial Distribution
- IP Addresses
- Malware
- Brute Force Attacks
- MITM (Man-In-The-Middle) Attacks
- DDoS (Distributed Denial of Service) Attacks
- Heatmap Visualization
- Exploratory Data Analysis (EDA)
- Ethical Implications
- Privacy and Confidentiality

4.11   Review Questions

1. What is an IP address?
   An IP address (Internet Protocol address) is a numerical label assigned to each device connected to a computer network that uses the Internet Protocol for communication.

2. What is Malware?
   Malware is malicious software designed to disrupt, damage, or gain unauthorized access to computer systems.

3. What are Brute Force attacks?
   Brute Force attacks are trial-and-error methods used to decode encrypted data such as passwords by systematically checking all possible combinations.

4. What is a MITM (Man-In-The-Middle) attack?
   A MITM attack is a cyberattack where the attacker secretly intercepts and relays messages between two parties who believe they are directly communicating with each other.

5. What is a DDoS (Distributed Denial of Service) attack?
   A DDoS attack is a malicious attempt to disrupt the normal traffic of a targeted server, service, or network by overwhelming it with a flood of Internet traffic from multiple sources.

6. What is heatmap visualization?

Heatmap visualization is a graphical representation of data where values are depicted by color, often used to show the density or intensity of data points in a geographic area or within a matrix.

7. What is Exploratory Data Analysis (EDA)?

EDA is an approach to analyzing datasets with the goal to summarize their main characteristics, often with visual methods, before making any assumptions.

8. What are the ethical implications of data analysis?

The ethical implications of data analysis include concerns about privacy, consent, data security, bias in data collection and interpretation, and the potential for misuse of data.

9. What are the concerns regarding privacy and confidentiality in data analysis?

Concerns include the risk of unauthorized access to sensitive data, ensuring data is anonymized, and maintaining confidentiality to protect individuals' identities and personal information.

10. How can one mitigate the risks associated with Brute Force Attacks?

Mitigation strategies include using strong, complex passwords, implementing account lockout mechanisms after multiple failed attempts, and utilizing two-factor authentication.

11. What is the importance of reviewing questions in data analysis?

Reviewing questions helps ensure that the analysis addresses the right problems, that the methods used are appropriate, and that the conclusions drawn are valid and reliable.

4.12   Suggested Websites

• Kaggle – [www.kaggle.com]: Data science and machine learning platform.

- Towards Data Science – [https://towardsdatascience.com]: A Medium publication sharing concepts, ideas, and codes.
- DataCamp – [www.datacamp.com]: Enables learning data science online.
- The Jupyter Project – [https://jupyter.org].
- Google Colab – [https://colab.google].
- R-bloggers – [www.r-bloggers.com]: A blog aggregator focused on R programming and data analysis.
- StatQuest – [https://statquest.org]: A YouTube channel offering clear and engaging tutorials on statistics and data analysis.

5

THE CYBERSECURITY MODEL DESIGN

5.1 The Cybersecurity Model Design

In this chapter, we examine the cybersecurity model design, which includes an organized approach to systematically addressing potential threats and vulnerabilities within a digital infrastructure. This process begins with a clear problem definition (Chapter 4), which lays the foundation for identifying the specific security challenges that need to be solved. Based on the guidance data science lifecycle roadmap introduced in Chapter 2, model design represents the following question: what's our approach?

Our approach integrates defined problems, exploratory data analysis (EDA) results, and cautious preprocessing of the data for model design (Figure 5.1). Model design and development in the context of machine learning (ML) or data science typically involve a series of interconnected steps. These steps are key in designing and building a strong cybersecurity model that can handle and mitigate threats effectively. Feature selection and engineering play an important role in designing and refining the model. Through the identification and selection of the relevant features, the model is handled precisely and efficiently.

5.2 What's Our Approach?

Machine learning algorithms are the foundation of our cybersecurity model. The choice of the appropriate algorithm is impacted by the problem definition, the type of data, and the specific security

DOI: 10.1201/9781003631514-5

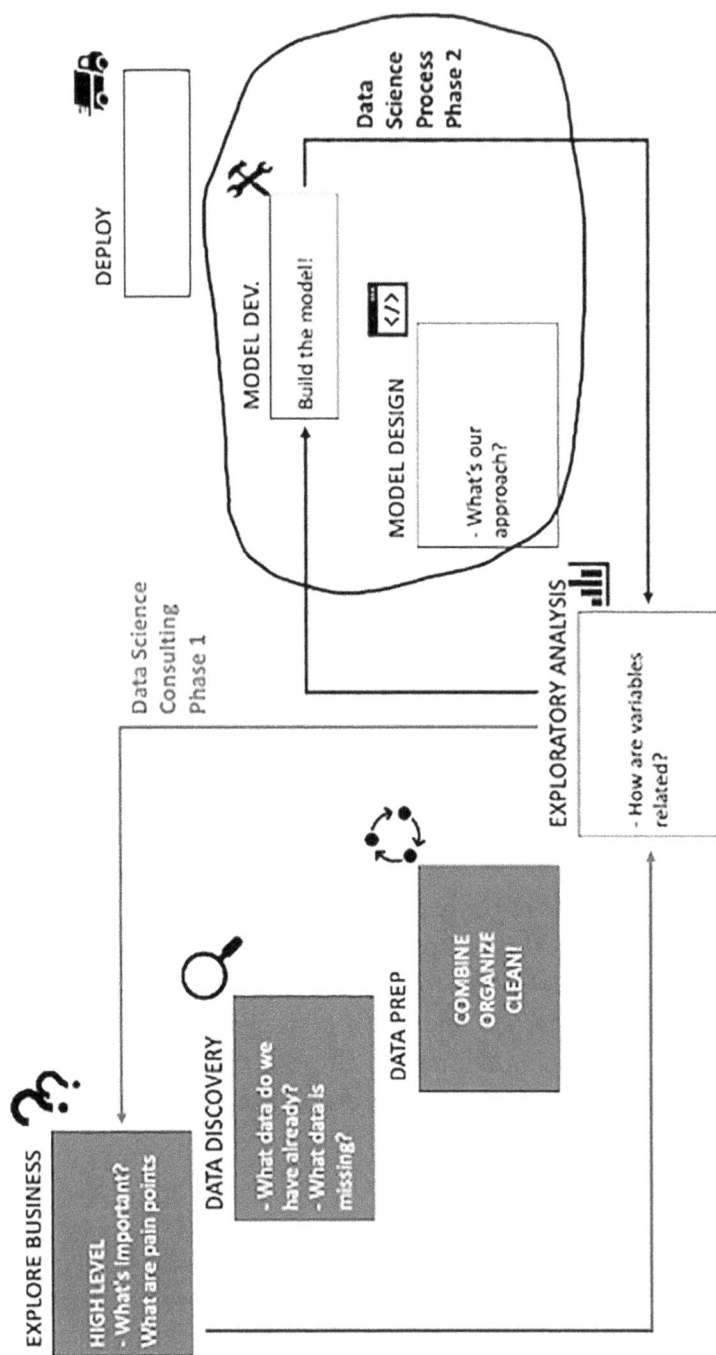

Figure 5.1 Data science lifecycle roadmap.

requirements. Certain algorithms (decision trees, random forests, support vector machines, and neural networks) are usually used in cybersecurity applications. The mentioned algorithms have their strengths and weaknesses; the selection varies depending on different factors (accuracy, interpretability, and computational efficiency). Once a the particular algorithm is chosen, the next step involves training the model using historical data. This covers splitting the data into training and testing sets, tuning hyperparameters if needed, and evaluating the model's performance (precision, recall, F1-score, and AUC-ROC). The final phase of the model design process involves deployment and continuous monitoring, which will be covered in Chapters 6 and 7. A structured approach to machine learning (ML) model design based on our IIoT-WSN Cyber Threats dataset is elaborated upon in the following sections.

5.3 Problem Definition

The increasing cyber threats targeting IIoT and WSN infrastructures pose significant risks to industrial systems. This predictive cybersecurity project aims to design a predictive model that can classify and detect potential cyberattacks based on sensor and network telemetry data (IIoT-WSN Cyber Threats dataset). The vital objective is to develop a robust machine learning model that accurately identifies malicious activity patterns and attack types. The model should be capable of recognizing patterns and trends that are indicative of such attacks.

5.4 Understanding EDA Results

The EDA analysis results in Chapter 4 are as follows:

- Attack Trends: The time-series analysis highlighted variations in attack occurrences, with anomalies detected at specific time intervals.
- Geospatial Attack Sources: A heatmap visualizes the attack origin distribution, indicating high-risk geographic zones.
- Feature Distributions: Numerical features (CPU usage, payload entropy, and memory usage) showed correlations with malicious activities.

- Feature Importance: Early correlation analysis indicated that packet size, temperature fluctuations, and request types could be relevant indicators of attack likelihood.

EDA insights lead us to refine our data preprocessing steps and select relevant features to improve model performance.

5.5 Data Preprocessing for Model Design

Before delving into the model training, some preprocessing steps must be implemented within our dataset, as shown in Figure 5.2. In the following part of this section, we will conduct hands-on research and run prepared Python scripting, which will guide us through the data preprocessing steps.

Step 1: Handling Missing Values, where it drops rows where "Attack_Type" is missing to ensure all samples are labeled; it also fills in missing values in numerical columns, using the median to avoid bias from extreme values.

```
import pandas as pd

# Load dataset
df = pd.read_csv('/content/drive/MyDrive/
Colab Notebooks/2nd Book AtBu/IIoT-WSN_
CyberThreats.csv')

# Drop rows where 'Attack_Type' is missing
(if necessary)
df = df.dropna(subset=['Attack_Type'])

# Fill missing values in numerical columns
with their median values
df.fillna(df.median(numeric_only=True),
inplace=True)

# Display updated dataset info
print(df.info())
```

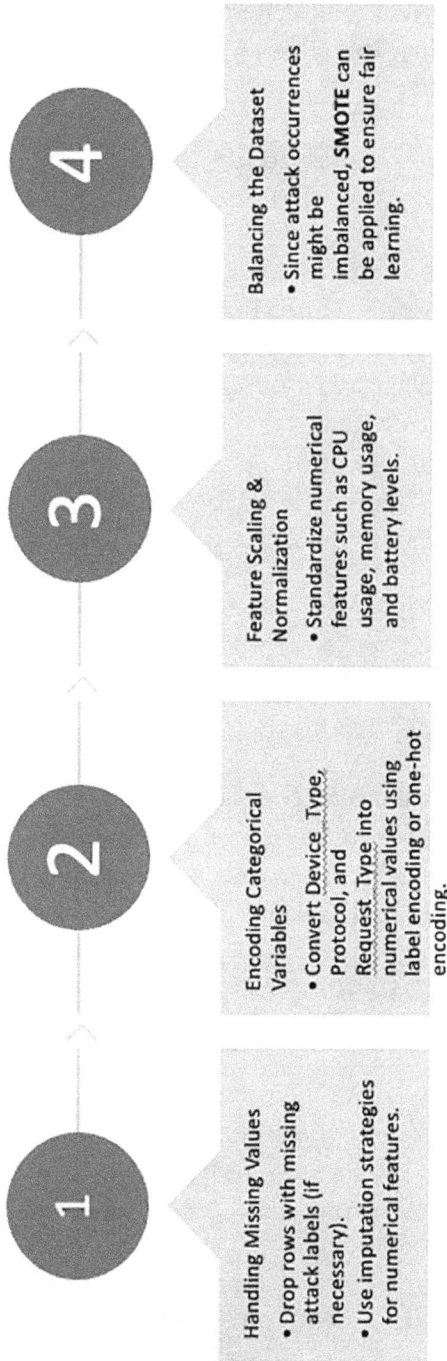

Figure 5.2 Data preprocessing steps.

Step 2: Encoding Categorical Variables, where it converts categorical columns (Device_Type, Protocol, Request_Type) into numerical values using Label Encoding. This allows ML models to process categorical data efficiently.

```
from sklearn.preprocessing import
LabelEncoder, OneHotEncoder

# Encoding categorical features
label_encoder = LabelEncoder()
df['Device_Type'] = label_encoder.fit_
transform(df['Device_Type'])
df['Protocol'] = label_encoder.fit_
transform(df['Protocol'])
df['Request_Type'] = label_encoder.fit_
transform(df['Request_Type'])

# Display the first few rows to verify
encoding
print(df[['Device_Type', 'Protocol',
'Request_Type']].head())
```

Step 3: Feature Scaling & Normalization, where StandardScaler normalizes numerical features to have zero mean and unit variance, improving model stability. It ensures that features like Packet Size, CPU Usage, and Battery Level are on the same scale.

```
from sklearn.preprocessing import
StandardScaler

# Select numerical features for scaling
num_features = ['Packet_Size', 'Payload_
Entropy', 'CPU_Usage (%)', 'Memory_Usage
(%)', 'Temperature (°C)', 'Battery_Level
(%)']

# Standardize numerical features
scaler = StandardScaler()
```

```
df[num_features] = scaler.fit_
transform(df[num_features])

# Display the first few rows to verify
scaling
print(df[num_features].head())
```

Step 4: Balancing the Dataset, where SMOTE generates synthetic samples for the minority class. It ensures equal representation of attack types, preventing bias in model training.

```
from imblearn.over_sampling import SMOTE

# Define features and labels
X = df.drop(columns=['Attack_Type']) #
Features
y = df['Attack_Type'] # Target variable

# Apply SMOTE to balance the classes
smote = SMOTE(random_state=42)
X_resampled, y_resampled = smote.fit_
resample(X, y)

# Convert back to DataFrame
df_resampled = pd.DataFrame(X_resampled,
columns=X.columns)
df_resampled['Attack_Type'] = y_resampled

# Check class distribution after balancing
print(df_resampled['Attack_Type'].value_
counts())
```

5.6 Feature Selection and Engineering

5.6.1 *Selection of the Most Relevant Features for the Model*

Based on EDA results and correlation analysis, the following features were selected for ML model training as the potential and most relevant ones. The chosen relevant features were then refined through feature engineering techniques (transforming variables, creating new interaction terms, and removing redundant features) to enhance their predictive power.

- **Packet Size**: Large packets may indicate anomalous behavior.
- **Payload Entropy**: Measures randomness in data, helping to detect encoded attacks.
- **CPU Usage (%)**: High CPU usage might be associated with certain DoS attacks.
- **Memory Usage (%)**: Memory spikes may be linked to malware infections.
- **Temperature (°C)**: Abnormal temperature changes could be linked to environmental attacks.
- **Battery Level (%)**: Important for WSN security as attackers may drain resources.
- **Request Type**: Specific commands (e.g., PUBLISH, POST) might be attack-prone.
- **Protocol Used**: Certain protocols (e.g., MQTT, CoAP) might be more vulnerable.

5.6.2   *Optional Features*

Additional features that might improve model performance but are optional include the following:

- **Source IP & Destination IP**: These could be used for IP reputation-based attack detection, but might introduce high cardinality issues.
- **Geographical Coordinates (Latitude, Longitude)**: If regional attack trends influence predictions, these can be included.
- **Anomaly Scores (from EDA)**: If an unsupervised anomaly detection model is run, its anomaly scores could be an additional feature.

5.7   Machine Learning Algorithms to be Used

We will examine multiple ML models for cyberattack prediction and choose the best-performing one using our dataset (Table 5.1).

TABLE 5.1   Multiple ML Models for Cyberattack Prediction

ALGORITHM	REASON FOR SELECTION
Logistic Regression	Baseline classifier for binary classification (attack/no attack).
Random Forest (RF)	Robust in handling mixed data types and feature importance evaluation.
Gradient Boosting (XGBoost, LightGBM)	High accuracy with feature interaction learning.
Support Vector Machine (SVM)	Effective in small datasets with clear decision boundaries.
Neural Networks (MLPClassifier)	To explore deep learning's ability in pattern recognition.

In the sections of Chapter 6, we will conduct hands-on research and run prepared Python scripting, which will guide us through the implementation of feature engineering and preprocessing; we will train ML models and evaluate performance based on accuracy, precision, recall, and F1-score.

5.8   Summary

This chapter discusses a hands-on approach that advances our understanding of how machine learning is used to predict cyberattacks. Also, we focus on empowering readers of this book with the skills needed to build and tune their predictive models, benefiting from the strengths of each used algorithm. The chapter highlights the importance of feature engineering and preprocessing, training ML models, and evaluating their performance (accuracy, precision, recall, and F1-score).

5.9   Key Terms

- Feature Engineering
- Preprocessing
- Accuracy
- Precision
- Recall
- F1-score
- Support Vector Machine (SVM)
- Neural Networks (MLPClassifier)

5.10   Review Questions

1. What is the primary objective of model design in cybersecurity for IIoT and WSNs?

   The primary objective is to develop a structured machine learning model capable of detecting malicious activities and anomalies in IIoT and WSN environments while ensuring high accuracy and low false positive rates.

2. Why is feature selection critical in model design?

   Feature selection is essential to eliminate irrelevant or redundant variables, improve model performance, and reduce computational complexity while focusing on the most informative attributes.

3. What are the key steps in Exploratory Data Analysis (EDA)?
   Key steps include:

   • Checking data distributions.
   • Identifying missing values and outliers.
   • Analyzing feature correlations.
   • Visualizing relationships among variables.

4. How does class imbalance affect machine learning models in cybersecurity?

   Class imbalance can lead to biased models, where the classifier favors the majority class, reducing the ability to detect rare cyberattacks. Techniques like SMOTE (Synthetic Minority Over-sampling Technique) can help balance the dataset.

5. What preprocessing steps are required for IIoT and WSN datasets?

   Handling missing values.

   Feature scaling and normalization.

   Encoding categorical variables.

   Splitting data into training and testing sets.

6. What role do feature engineering and transformation play in model design?

   Feature engineering helps create more relevant variables by transforming existing data and improving model predictions through domain-specific knowledge.

7. What are the challenges of designing ML models for IIoT and WSN security?
   Challenges include:
   - High-dimensional data.
   - Limited labeled attack data.
   - Latency and resource constraints in IIoT devices.
   - Evolving attack patterns.

8. How do we select the appropriate machine learning algorithm?
   The selection depends on:
   - Data type (structured/unstructured).
   - Feature complexity.
   - Computational efficiency.
   - Model interpretability.

9. What is the importance of hyperparameter tuning in model design?
   Hyperparameter tuning optimizes model performance by adjusting parameters like learning rate, tree depth, and regularization, ensuring better generalization.

10. Why is model validation essential before deployment?
   Validation prevents overfitting, ensuring the model performs well on new data, rather than just the training dataset.

11. How do we evaluate the designed model before implementation?
   By using metrics like:
   - Confusion Matrix (TP, TN, FP, FN).
   - Precision, Recall, F1-score.
   - ROC-AUC Curve.

5.11   Suggested Websites

- Scikit-learn Documentation – [https://scikit-learn.org/stable/].
- Kaggle – Cybersecurity Datasets – [www.kaggle.com/datasets].
- IBM Machine Learning Fundamentals – [www.ibm.com/cloud/learn/machine-learning].
- Feature Selection Techniques – [https://towardsdatascience.com/feature-selection].
- Data Preprocessing in ML – [www.datacamp.com/blog/data-preprocessing/].

6

THE AI ML MODEL DEVELOPMENT FOR IIoT AND WSN SECURITY

6.1 The AI ML Model Development for IIoT and WSN Security

In this chapter, we investigate the development of an AI-driven machine learning (ML) model designed for enhancing cybersecurity in the Industrial Internet of Things (IIoT) and wireless sensor networks (WSNs). Given the increasing integration of smart devices and connected systems in industrial applications, security threats have become more sophisticated, making intelligent threat detection systems essential. The primary goal of this chapter is to introduce a structured approach to building, training, and evaluating an ML model capable of identifying malicious activity patterns in IIoT-WSN environments. This chapter discusses the challenges encountered during model development, particularly class imbalance issues, and potential solutions such as oversampling techniques, cost-sensitive learning, or alternative ML approaches. Based on the guidance data science lifecycle roadmap introduced in Chapter 2 (Figure 6.1), model development represents the following task: build the model!

6.2 Build the Model

The model development phase is a vital step in designing an effective machine learning model capable of detecting cyberthreats within IIoT-WSN environments. In this phase, we designed and implemented a random forest classifier, selected due to its ability to handle mixed data types and provide feature importance insights.

DOI: 10.1201/9781003631514-6

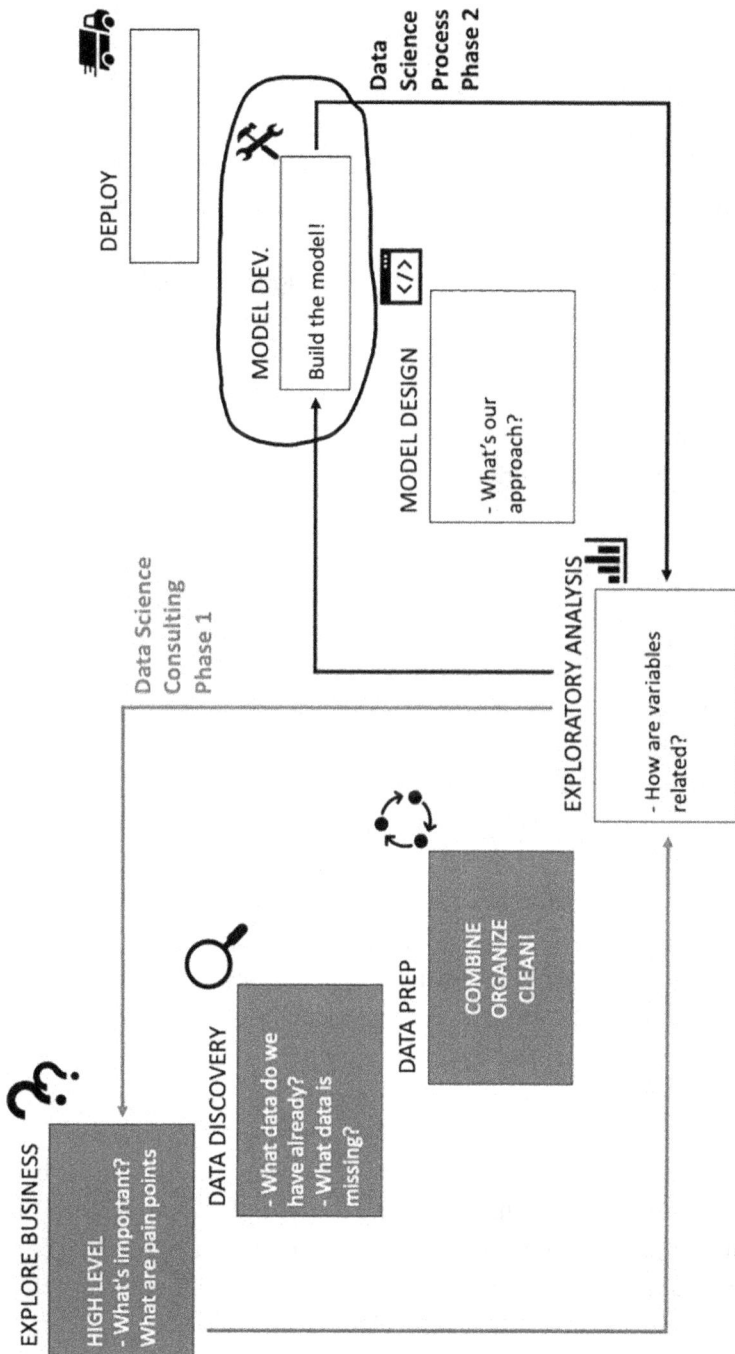

Figure 6.1 Data science lifecycle roadmap.

The dataset went through extensive preprocessing, including feature selection, class balancing strategies, and the transformation of categorical variables into numerical representations. Despite these efforts, initial evaluations highlighted challenges related to class imbalance, leading to difficulties in accurately identifying malicious activity. This outcome indicates the necessity of refining the feature selection strategy and improving the representation of attack instances in the training dataset.

The model's architecture will need continuous fine-tuning, ensuring that it is not only accurate but also resilient against cyber threats in IIoT-WSN infrastructures. This systematic development process aims to bridge the gap between theoretical cybersecurity principles and practical model implementation, enhancing predictive accuracy and security response capabilities.

6.3   Objective Definition

The primary objective of this model development is to build a robust machine learning model capable of accurately detecting malicious activity and attack types within industrial IoT and WSNs. Given the increasing intricacy of cyberthreats targeting critical infrastructures, the model is designed to analyze network- and sensor-based anomalies, recognizing distinct behavioral patterns that indicate potential intrusions. The goal is not only to achieve high accuracy in attack detection but also to minimize false positives, ensuring that legitimate network operations are not misclassified as threats.

To achieve this, the model must be adaptable, scalable, and capable of real-time threat detection. The feature selection process plays a crucial role in ensuring that the input data contains meaningful attributes that contribute to distinguishing between normal and attack scenarios. The incorporation of ensemble learning techniques, combined with data augmentation and advanced preprocessing, further strengthens the model's resilience. Ultimately, the success of this project will be measured by the model's ability to provide actionable intelligence, allowing security teams to proactively mitigate potential threats before they escalate into full-scale cyber incidents.

6.4   Feature Selection and Engineering

As we stated in Chapter 5, considering the EDA results and correlation analysis, the features ("Device_Type", "Protocol", "Packet_Size", "Request_Type", "Payload_Entropy", "CPU_Usage (%)", "Memory_Usage (%)", "Temperature (°C)", "Battery_Level (%)", and "Year") were selected for ML model training as the potential and most relevant ones. In this and the next section, we will conduct hands-on research and run prepared Python scripting, which will guide us through the implementation of feature engineering and preprocessing. We will train ML models and evaluate performance based on accuracy, precision, recall, and F1-score.

Step 1: Generating feature importance analysis – with the following script, here, we will build an accurate cyberattack detection model; we must select the most important features that contribute significantly to attack identification. To achieve this outcome, we will generate a feature importance analysis which will lead us further toward ML model development. The feature selection approach will include correlation analysis, feature importance (based on random forest/XGBoost algorithms), and evaluation of dependencies between features and target variables.

```
# Selection of the Most Relevant Features
for the Model
# Generating Feature Importance Analysis

import pandas as pd
import numpy as np
import matplotlib.pyplot as plt
import seaborn as sns
from sklearn.ensemble import
RandomForestClassifier
from sklearn.feature_selection import
mutual_info_classif
```

```
# Load the preprocessed dataset
file_path = "/content/drive/MyDrive/
Colab Notebooks/2nd Book AtBu/IIoT-WSN_
CyberThreats_preprocessed.csv"
df = pd.read_csv(file_path)

# Define features and target variable
X = df.drop(columns=['Malicious_Activity',
'Attack_Type', 'Device_ID', 'Source_IP',
'Destination_IP', 'Geo_Location'])
y = df['Malicious_Activity'] # Binary
classification target

# --- 1. Correlation Analysis ---
plt.figure(figsize=(12, 8))
sns.heatmap(X.corr(), annot=True, cmap=
"coolwarm", fmt=".2f", linewidths=0.5)
plt.title("Feature Correlation Heatmap")
plt.show()

# --- 2. Feature Importance using Random
Forest ---
rf_model = RandomForestClassifier(n_
estimators=100, random_state=42)
rf_model.fit(X, y)

# Extract feature importance
feature_importance =
pd.DataFrame({'Feature': X.columns,
'Importance': rf_model.feature_
importances_})
feature_importance = feature_importance.
sort_values(by="Importance", ascending=
False)

# Plot Feature Importance
plt.figure(figsize=(10, 6))
sns.barplot(x="Importance", y="Feature",
data=feature_importance)
```

```
plt.title("Feature Importance using Random
Forest")
plt.show()

# --- 3. Mutual Information Score ---
mi_scores = mutual_info_classif(X, y)
mi_scores_
df = pd.DataFrame({'Feature': X.columns,
'Mutual_Info_Score': mi_scores})
mi_scores_df = mi_scores_df.sort_
values(by="Mutual_Info_Score", ascending=
False)

# Display top features
print("Top Features Based on Mutual
Information:")
print(mi_scores_df.head(10))
# Select Top 8-10 Features for Model
Training

selected_features = feature_
importance["Feature"][:10].tolist()
print("Selected Features for Model:",
selected_features)
```

Figure 6.2 introduces the feature correlation analysis results, where relationships between variables are identified. Another good result from Step 1 was that we identified relevant features (Device_Type, Protocol, Packet_Size, Request_Type, Payload_Entropy, CPU_Usage (%), Memory_Usage (%), Temperature (°C), Battery_Level (%), and Year) that are vital for the next step in model development.

6.5 Machine Learning Model Selection

By examining multiple ML models for cyberattack prediction, we selected a minimum of two ML model algorithms for an accurate cyberattack detection model. At this moment, we move forward to model development by utilizing two algorithms, random forest

Feature Correlation Heatmap

	Device_Type	Protocol	Packet_Size	Request_Type	Payload_Entropy	CPU_Usage (%)	Memory_Usage (%)	Temperature (°C)	Battery_Level (%)	Year	Month	Day	Hour	Minute	Second
Device_Type	1.00	0.05	0.02	0.02	0.02	-0.01	0.03	0.04	-0.01	-0.01	0.01	-0.06	-0.03	0.03	
Protocol	0.05	1.00	-0.01	0.02	-0.00	-0.04	-0.04	0.03	0.03	-0.02	0.01	0.02	0.01	-0.00	
Packet_Size	0.02	-0.01	1.00	-0.02	-0.00	0.02	0.01	0.06	-0.03	-0.06	0.06	-0.02	-0.01	-0.02	
Request_Type	0.02	0.02	-0.02	1.00	0.03	-0.01	-0.02	-0.07	0.09	-0.06	0.06	0.01	0.03	-0.01	
Payload_Entropy	0.02	-0.00	-0.00	0.03	1.00	-0.08	-0.02	0.04	-0.03	0.04	-0.03	-0.03	0.02	-0.00	
CPU_Usage (%)	-0.01	-0.04	0.02	-0.01	-0.08	1.00	0.06	-0.01	0.05	0.03	-0.04	0.04	-0.01	-0.03	
Memory_Usage (%)	0.03	-0.04	0.01	-0.02	-0.02	0.06	1.00	-0.03	-0.03	-0.02	0.02	0.01	-0.03	-0.02	
Temperature (°C)	0.04	0.03	0.06	-0.07	0.04	-0.01	-0.03	1.00	-0.05	-0.04	0.04	0.04	-0.00	-0.03	
Battery_Level (%)	-0.01	0.03	-0.03	0.09	-0.03	0.05	-0.03	-0.05	1.00	-0.02	0.02	0.00	0.03	-0.02	
Year	-0.01	-0.02	-0.06	-0.06	0.04	0.03	-0.02	-0.04	-0.02	1.00	-0.98	-0.19	-0.01	0.05	
Month	0.01	0.01	0.06	0.06	-0.03	-0.04	0.02	0.04	0.02	0.98	1.00	0.15	0.02	-0.05	
Day	-0.06	0.02	-0.02	0.01	-0.03	0.04	0.01	0.04	0.00	-0.19	0.15	1.00	-0.01	0.06	
Hour	-0.03	0.01	-0.01	0.03	0.02	-0.01	-0.03	-0.00	0.03	-0.01	0.02	-0.01	1.00	-0.07	
Minute	0.03	-0.00	-0.02	-0.01	-0.00	-0.03	-0.02	-0.03	-0.02	0.05	-0.05	0.06	-0.07	1.00	
Second															

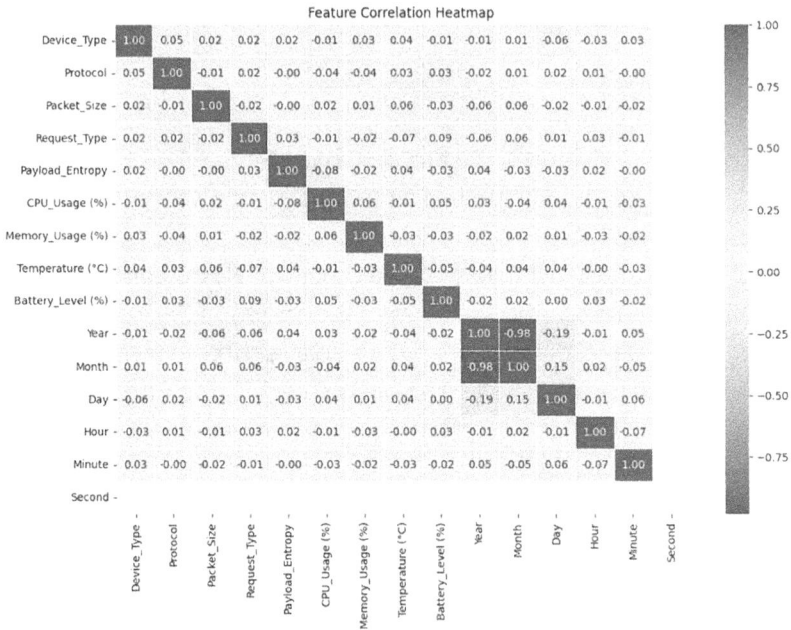

Figure 6.2 Feature correlation heatmap shows relationships between variables.

(RF) and gradient boosting (XGBoost). Based on the EDA results and our objective, we want our model to be able to accurately detect cyberattacks based on pattern recognition and trends, robust handling of data variability, and scalability for large datasets. The selection of a suitable machine learning model is a crucial aspect of this research, as it directly impacts the accuracy and efficiency of cyberattack detection in IIoT-WSN environments. The chosen models must be capable of handling high-dimensional data, processing real-time network traffic, and distinguishing between normal and malicious activities.

Random forest was selected as the potential model for the current implementation due to its high interpretability and resilience to overfitting. RF is well-suited for handling mixed data types, which is essential in IIoT-WSN environments where data originates from multiple heterogeneous sources, including sensor readings, network logs, and security event reports. However, challenges surfaced during the model training process due to the presence of imbalanced class distributions in the dataset. The model encountered difficulties in detecting minority class instances, leading to misleading performance metrics. The confusion matrix revealed that the model primarily predicted all samples as Normal (0), ignoring attack instances due to the lack of diverse attack data in the training set.

Overall, the model selection process highlights the need for continuous algorithm refinement, dataset enhancement, and feature engineering improvements. The current implementation using random forest serves as a baseline model, offering a structured approach to feature selection and attack classification.

6.6   Model Development

6.6.1   Training Process

The following script will load the preprocessed dataset and split data into sets (Train (80%) & Test (20%)), train two ML models based on selected algorithms, save training & testing data separately (CSV files), and evaluate the performance of the model. Once executed, we analyze which model performs better and choose that one for the further steps in Chapter 7.

6.6.2   Testing and Evaluation Process

After the train-test step occurs, the next step in the process of model development includes evaluating performance metrics (accuracy, precision, recall, F1-score). Afterward, depending on which model's performance behavior would exceed the other's, or if both would satisfy our objectives, we will move toward ML model deployment in Chapter 7.

Step 1: The next script will load the preprocessed dataset and split data into sets (Train (80%) & Test (20%)), train two ML models based on selected algorithms, save training & testing data separately (CSV files), and evaluate the performance of the model. After thorough testing, we couldn't manage the required results with the XGBoost algorithm, so we excluded it and moved with the Random Forest model.

```python
# Train ML Model (Random Forest Only) &
Save Results

import pandas as pd
import numpy as np
from sklearn.model_selection import train_
test_split
from sklearn.ensemble import
RandomForestClassifier
from sklearn.metrics import accuracy_
score, precision_score, recall_score, f1_
score
from imblearn.over_sampling import SMOTE

# Load the preprocessed dataset
file_path = "/content/drive/MyDrive/
Colab Notebooks/2nd Book AtBu/IIoT-WSN_
CyberThreats_preprocessed.csv"
df = pd.read_csv(file_path)

# Define Features (X) and Target
Variable (y)
selected_features = ['Device_Type',
'Protocol', 'Packet_Size', 'Request_Type',
'Payload_Entropy',
            'CPU_Usage (%)', 'Memory_Usage
(%)', 'Temperature (°C)', 'Battery_Level
(%)', 'Year']
X = df[selected_features]
y = df['Malicious_Activity']  # Target
variable (Attack vs. Normal)

# Check the class distribution of the
target variable (y)
print("Class distribution in target
variable (y):")
print(y.value_counts())
```

```python
# Train-Test Split (80% Training, 20%
Testing)
X_train, X_test, y_train, y_test = train_
test_split(X, y, test_size=0.2, random_
state=42, stratify=y)

# Check the class distribution in y_train
print("\nClass distribution in y_train
(after stratification):")
print(y_train.value_counts())

# Ensure y_train contains more than 1
unique value before applying SMOTE
if len(np.unique(y_train)) > 1:
  print("\n✅ Applying SMOTE to balance the
dataset...")
  smote = SMOTE(random_state=42)
  X_train, y_train = smote.fit_resample(X_
train, y_train)

  # Check class distribution after SMOTE
  print("\nClass distribution in y_train
after SMOTE:")
  print(y_train.value_counts())

else:
  print("\n✅ Skipping SMOTE: Only one
class detected in y_train.")
  print("Check the dataset to ensure there
are both 0s and 1s before training.")

# Save Train and Test Sets as CSV
train_file = "/content/drive/MyDrive/Colab
Notebooks/2nd Book AtBu/IIoT-WSN_Train.
csv"
test_file = "/content/drive/MyDrive/Colab
Notebooks/2nd Book AtBu/IIoT-WSN_Test.csv"
```

```python
pd.concat([X_train, y_train], axis=1).to_
csv(train_file, index=False)
pd.concat([X_test, y_test], axis=1).to_
csv(test_file, index=False)
print(f"\nTrain dataset saved: {train_
file}")
print(f"Test dataset saved: {test_file}")

# Initialize Random Forest Model
rf_model = RandomForestClassifier(n_
estimators=100, random_state=42)

# Train Random Forest Model
rf_model.fit(X_train, y_train)

# Predictions
y_pred_rf = rf_model.predict(X_test)

# Evaluate Performance
def evaluate_model(y_true, y_pred, model_
name):
  accuracy = accuracy_score(y_true, y_pred)
  precision = precision_score(y_true, y_
pred, zero_division=1)
  recall = recall_score(y_true, y_pred,
zero_division=1)
  f1 = f1_score(y_true, y_pred, zero_
division=1)
  print(f"\n✅ {model_name} Performance:")
  print(f"✅ Accuracy: {accuracy:.4f}")
  print(f"✅ Precision: {precision:.4f}")
  print(f"✅ Recall: {recall:.4f}")
  print(f"✅ F1-Score: {f1:.4f}")

# Display Metrics for Random Forest Model
evaluate_model(y_test, y_pred_rf, "Random
Forest")
```

6.7   Generate Results

Our model achieved perfect performance (100% Accuracy, Precision, Recall, and F1-score), which usually means one of two things: if your dataset is very small or simple, that's okay, and any overfitting or data leakage could occur. If the dataset is naturally easy to classify, a perfect score is possible. However, you should still validate with real-world data to ensure generalization and applicability for the business case you had to work on. Sometimes, overfitting means that the model memorizes the training data instead of learning real patterns; also, data leakage where the model might be learning from unintended features (e.g., ID fields, timestamp patterns, or labels leaking into features). All those potential challenges or issues during model development need to be considered whenever you work on real-world cases. In this book, we want to bring all kinds of example cases since they're not real-world scenarios so that you would understand the position you find yourself in.

6.8   Data Visualization

Figure 6.3 will provide insight into how well the model distinguishes between malicious (1) and normal (0) activities. A Various visualization can be used to present the behavior and performance of the ML model; each provides a certain way of interpretation.

6.9   Data Interpretation

The evaluation of the machine learning model for cyberattack detection highlights key challenges and areas for improvement. The confusion matrix indicates that the model consistently predicts only one class—Normal (0)—and fails to classify any Malicious (1) instances. This suggests a strong class imbalance or bias in the training process, resulting in a model that does not generalize well to malicious activity detection.

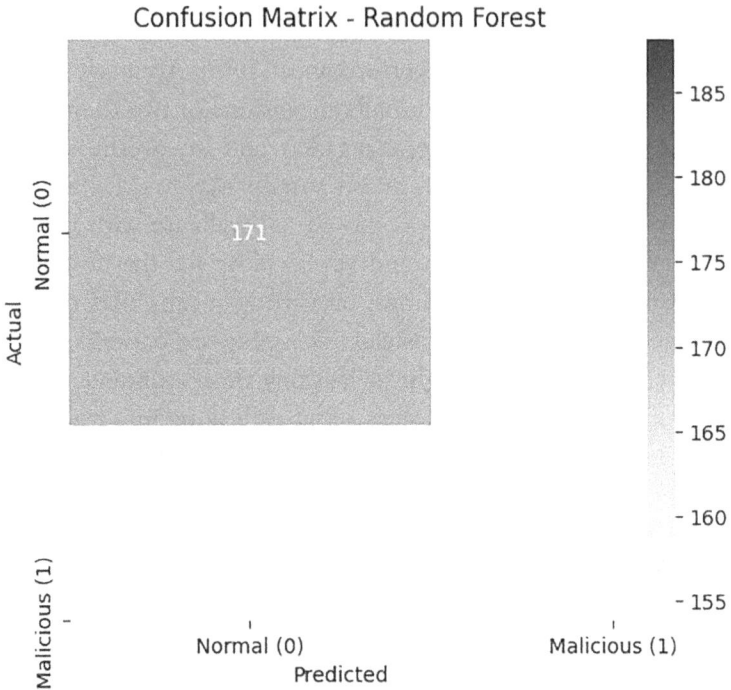

Figure 6.3 Confusion matrix for random forest.

Many factors may have contributed to these results:

- **Class Imbalance:** The dataset predominantly contains normal traffic, leading the model to prioritize normal activity over detecting attacks. This imbalance prevents effective learning of attack patterns.
- **Model Bias:** The random forest classifier, despite being robust, may have learned an overly simplistic decision boundary that does not differentiate between attack and normal behavior.
- **Feature Relevance:** The selected features may not provide enough discriminatory power to distinguish between attack types effectively. A deeper analysis of feature importance and correlation is necessary.
- **Insufficient Training Data for Attacks:** If the training set contains very few malicious instances, the model may struggle to recognize them.

But we always learn from such outcomes, which fail to include a well-balanced ML model development. Don't worry, let's assess and think about what potential recommendations and next steps we can follow to mitigate. To improve model performance and align with the project's objective—building a robust machine learning model capable of accurately detecting malicious activity patterns and attack types— the following steps should be considered:

- **Class Balance Adjustment**: Implement SMOTE (Synthetic Minority Over-sampling Technique) or acquire a more balanced dataset.
- **Feature Selection Refinement**: Analyze and select the most critical features that contribute to attack detection.
- **Alternative Algorithms**: Explore other ML models such as XGBoost or neural networks (MLPClassifier), which may better capture complex attack patterns.
- **Reassessment of Label Distribution**: Ensure both training and test sets contain representative instances of both attack and normal traffic.
- **Additional Data Augmentation and Anomaly Detection Methods**: Consider incorporating unsupervised learning methods such as isolation forests or autoencoders for anomaly detection in cases where labeled attack data is scarce.

These improvements will help achieve the key objective of developing a machine learning model that effectively recognizes patterns and trends indicative of cyberthreats, improving overall cybersecurity resilience in IIoT-WSN systems.

6.10 Summary

This chapter presented the development and evaluation of an ML model for cyberthreat detection in IIoT and WSN systems. We highlighted the modeling process, from feature selection and data preprocessing to training and evaluation using random forest (RF). The model's performance was assessed using metrics such as accuracy, precision, recall, and F1-score, supported by visualizations such as confusion matrices.

6.11   Key Terms

- IIoT (Industrial Internet of Things)
- WSNs (Wireless Sensor Networks)
- Cyberthreat Detection
- SMOTE (Synthetic Minority Over-sampling Technique)
- Feature Selection
- Random Forest (RF)
- Accuracy
- Precision
- Recall
- F1-score
- Confusion Matrix
- XGBoost
- Neural Networks (MLPClassifier)
- Isolation Forests
- Autoencoders

6.12   Review Questions

1. What are the key steps in model development for IIoT and WSN security?
   The process includes:
   - Data preprocessing.
   - Feature selection and engineering.
   - Training and validation.
   - Performance evaluation.

2. How does supervised learning help in cybersecurity model development?
   Supervised learning utilizes labeled data to train models in detecting attacks, making it effective for known cyberthreats.

3. What are the benefits of using Random Forest for attack detection?
   Handles high-dimensional data well.

   Provides feature importance ranking.

   Robust to overfitting.

4. Why was XGBoost excluded from the final model selection?
   Due to class imbalance issues and training data constraints, XGBoost was removed to ensure a simpler and more interpretable approach using random forest.

5. How do we handle missing values in IIoT and WSN data?
   By using techniques such as:

   • Mean/median imputation.
   • Forward-filling missing values.
   • Removing incomplete data points.

6. What is the purpose of data stratification during train-test splitting?
   Stratification ensures that the class distribution remains balanced, preventing bias in the training data.

7. How can we validate model performance?
   By using techniques like:

   • Cross-validation.
   • Holdout validation.
   • Bootstrapping.

8. What are the advantages of using confusion matrices in evaluation?
   Confusion matrices provide insights into true positive, false positive, false negative, and true negative rates, helping to refine model accuracy.

9. Why is the ROC-AUC curve an essential metric?
   It shows the model's ability to differentiate between classes, with higher AUC indicating a better classification performance.

10. What are the next steps after model development?
    • Model testing in a simulated environment.
    • Performance optimization.
    • Deployment in a real-time setting.

11. What role does continuous learning play in ML-based cybersecurity models?
    Continuous learning enables models to adapt to evolving cyberthreats, improving detection accuracy over time.

6.13   Suggested Websites

- Random Forest Algorithm Guide – [https://towardsdatascie nce.com/the-random-forest-algorithm].
- Imbalanced Data Handling (SMOTE) – [https://imbalan ced-learn.org/stable/over_sampling.html].
- XGBoost Documentation – [https://xgboost.readthedocs.io/ en/latest/.
- ROC-AUC Explained – [https://scikit-learn.org/stable/ modules/generated/sklearn.metrics.roc_auc_score.html].
- Machine Learning for Cybersecurity – [www.dhs.gov/scie nce-and-technology/publication/cisa-advanced-analytics-platform-machine-learning-fact-sheet

7

THE CYBERSECURITY
MODEL DEPLOYMENT

7.1   The Cybersecurity Model Deployment

In this chapter, we examine the deployment of an ML model designed to enhance the cybersecurity of the IIoT and WSNs. The deployment phase ensures that the model is not only functional in an experimental setup but also integrated into real-world applications. A vital aspect of deployment includes building a web interface to provide user accessibility and real-time predictions. This process involves selecting the right infrastructure and ensuring security, scalability, and ease of use while addressing potential industry-specific requirements. In this chapter, the following sections will go through the process of building and developing the web interface, integrating APIs, and hosting the model on a cloud platform for secure and efficient deployment.

Based on the guidance data science lifecycle roadmap introduced in Chapter 2 (Figure 7.1), model deployment represents the task of developing the web interface, integrating APIs, and hosting the model.

7.2   Challenges and Best Practices

There are various challenges and best practices within this approach of deploying an AI-powered cybersecurity model. Important challenges that need to be considered and overcome include scalability, security, latency, model drift, and resource constraints. We need to consider scalability to make sure that the system can handle large-scale networks of IIoT and WSNs. Defense and prevention models eliminate attacks and threats from malicious actors. Small devices like IIoT have limitations when it comes to computational power, which is needed for lightweight

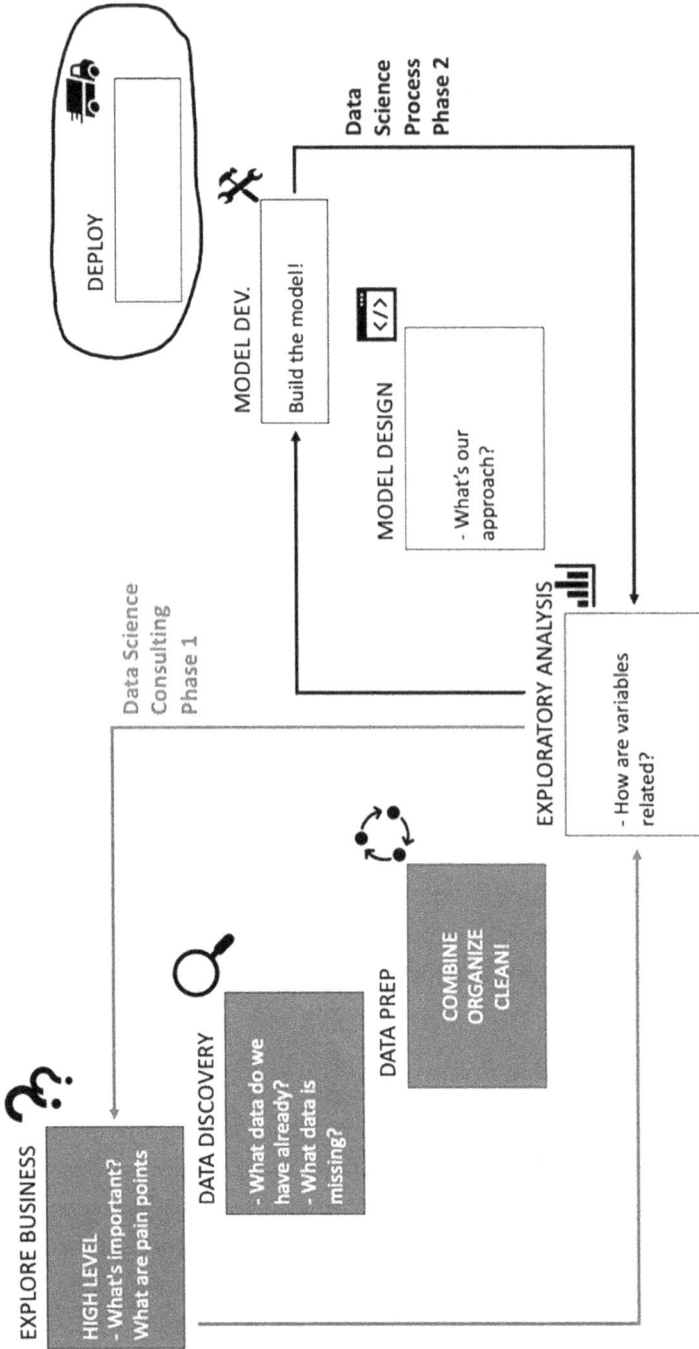

Figure 7.1 Data science lifecycle roadmap.

and efficient models. On the other hand, best practices include utilizing and benefiting from technology development. Use of containerization, for example, Docker, eases the integration of API-based access, enables continuous monitoring, provides updates to prevent model degradation, and secures the deployment with encryption controls.

7.3   Tools and Frameworks

Deploying an ML-based cybersecurity model for IIoT and WSNs requires a robust and scalable infrastructure. The deployment phase is where the trained model is transformed into an applicable, real-time cybersecurity solution that can detect and prevent cyberthreats across different industrial environments. To achieve this, several key tools and frameworks play a crucial role in ensuring efficient deployment, accessibility, and security. The following Table 7.1 tools and frameworks are widely used for deploying AI cybersecurity models.

The Flask and FastAPI frameworks serve as the foundation of model deployment by offering a lightweight, efficient API layer. These frameworks allow the trained cybersecurity model to be exposed as a RESTful API, enabling external systems, dashboards, and applications to interact with it. This supports deployment in various ways, including:

- Providing a structured way to send input data (network logs, attack features) and receive predictions.
- Ensuring real-time attack detection by allowing IoT devices and IIoT gateways to query the model remotely.

Table 7.1   Tools and Frameworks to Deploy the ML Model

CATEGORY	TOOL/FRAMEWORK	PURPOSE
Web API Framework	Flask / FastAPI	Lightweight web framework for serving ML models via REST APIs.
Model Serving	TensorFlow Serving	Used for deploying deep learning models efficiently.
Containerization	Docker	Containerization tool for consistent deployment across different environments.
Cloud Hosting	Heroku/AWS Lambda	Cloud hosting for deploying AI models as microservices.
Web Visualization	Streamlit/Dash	Python-based frameworks for building interactive web applications.

- FastAPI is optimized for asynchronous processing, reducing response times for high-volume requests.

For deep learning-based cybersecurity models, TensorFlow Serving ensures efficient and scalable deployment. If the model relies on neural networks for anomaly detection, this tool optimizes inference speed and supports dynamic model updates without downtime. It supports deployment in various ways, including:

- Optimized inference engine for handling large-scale traffic in IIoT/WSN networks.
- Scalable and updatable – The model can be retrained and reloaded dynamically without affecting operations.
- Works well with edge computing devices, reducing latency in security-critical applications.

Docker ensures that the deployed model and its dependencies are packaged in a lightweight, isolated container, making it easier to deploy across cloud, edge, and on-premises systems. This supports deployment in various ways, including:

- Eliminates dependency conflicts – The cybersecurity model works consistently across different environments.
- Enhances security – Running the model in isolated containers minimizes vulnerabilities.
- Allows rapid scaling – Containers can be deployed across multiple industrial IoT gateways or cloud servers.

Deploying the cybersecurity model in the cloud ensures global accessibility and scalability. Heroku is ideal for simple API hosting, while AWS Lambda provides a serverless, pay-per-use model, making it suitable for cost-efficient deployment. This supports deployment in various ways, including:

- Reduces infrastructure management – No need to maintain physical servers.
- Provides global accessibility – Organizations can query the cybersecurity model from anywhere.
- Scales based on demand – AWS Lambda automatically adjusts resources, ensuring low-latency detection during cyberattacks.

To enhance usability and industry adoption, the cybersecurity model needs an intuitive, interactive dashboard. Streamlit and Dash allow the model's predictions to be visualized through real-time security dashboards, alerting industry professionals to potential cyber-threats. This supports deployment in various ways, including:

- Provides real-time attack visualizations – Helps security teams monitor cyberthreats effectively.
- Allows user-friendly interaction – Security analysts can upload logs, adjust parameters, and view reports.
- Supports seamless API integration – Can be linked with Flask APIs or cloud-based ML models for live updates.

The combination of tools and frameworks ensures that the IIoT and WSN cybersecurity model is accessible, scalable, and effective. These tools enable the model to continuously detect, prevent, and report cyberthreats, making industrial IoT security more resilient against evolving cyberattacks.

7.4 How to Build a Cybersecurity Model Product

7.4.1 Design a Web Interface

A user-friendly web interface is key to interacting with the deployed cybersecurity model. The interface should allow security professionals to submit network logs, view real-time attack detections, and analyze historical attack trends. Some of the key features of the web interface include:

- File Upload: Users can upload network logs for real-time threat analysis.
- Live Attack Detection Dashboard: Visualizes detected cyberattacks using heatmaps and anomaly graphs.
- Authentication & Security: Ensures only authorized users can access the system.

The web interface will be built using Flask (backend) and Dash Streamlit (frontend visualization), ensuring a lightweight yet powerful interactive security dashboard.

In the following part of this section, we will examine a guide on how to develop the web interface, integrate APIs, and host the model on a cloud platform for secure and efficient deployment.

Step 1: Web interface implementation will initiate the process of model deployment. To make the cybersecurity model deployment functional and user-accessible, a web-based interface must be developed. This interface will allow security analysts, administrators, and industrial system operators to interact with the deployed model, analyze incoming network logs, and monitor cyberthreats. From a tech stack which we need on the backend to support the infrastructure running this model, we include:

- Backend: Flask or FastAPI (to expose the trained model as an API).
- Frontend: Streamlit, Dash, or React.js (for visualization of attack data).
- Database: PostgreSQL or Firebase (for storing logs and model outputs).

Step 2: API development and model integration, which make the cybersecurity model accessible, must be deployed as an API that external applications can communicate with. RESTful APIs will allow integration with firewalls, SIEM tools, and industrial control systems. Steps to develop such an API include:

- Load the trained ML Model (e.g., RandomForestClassifier trained on IIoT data).
- Create API Endpoints:
  - /predict: Receives input data and returns attack predictions.
  - /upload: Accepts network log files for batch processing.
- Secure API Requests:
  - Use JWT authentication and HTTPS encryption to prevent unauthorized access.
- Deploy API using Docker to ensure scalability and compatibility.

A code example of an API endpoint based on Flask is shown here:

```
from flask import Flask, request, jsonify

import joblib
import pandas as pd

app = Flask(__name__)
model = joblib.load("rf_model.pkl") # Load
trained ML model

@app.route('/predict', methods=['POST'])
def predict():
  data = request.json
  df = pd.DataFrame(data)
  prediction = model.predict(df)
  return jsonify({"prediction": prediction.
tolist()})

if __name__ == '__main__':
app.run(debug=True)
```

This API will allow real-time threat detection for industrial IoT and WSN networks.

Step 3: Real-time threat monitoring and alerts are crucial to this process. Once the cybersecurity model is deployed, it should provide real-time alerts for detected attacks. The system will be able to send email and SMS notifications to security teams, SIEM integration, dashboard indicators, etc. The tech stack used for the functionality of real-time monitoring could include:

- Kafka (for streaming network logs to the ML model).
- Elasticsearch and Kibana (for threat visualization).
- Prometheus and Grafana (for real-time monitoring dashboards).

This implementation will help and guide organizations to respond immediately to security incidents and mitigate cyberthreats before they escalate.

Table 7.2   Industry Application Cybersecurity Model Deployed

INDUSTRY	APPLICATION
Smart Cities	Real-time traffic control and surveillance system security.
Industrial Automation	Protection of SCADA systems and manufacturing control networks.
Healthcare IoT	Security of connected medical devices and hospital networks.
Critical Infrastructure	Cybersecurity monitoring for power grids, water supply networks, and oil refineries.

Step 4: Deployment in edge and cloud environments will conclude the process of model deployment. The cybersecurity model can be deployed in two primary environments:

- Cloud Deployment (AWS, Azure, or Google Cloud).
- Edge Deployment (On-premises or Industrial Gateway).

Additionally, the hybrid deployment model combines cloud-based centralized monitoring and edge-based local detection for optimal cybersecurity coverage.

7.4.2   *Serve the Industry*

The deployed cybersecurity model is designed to serve multiple industries that rely on IIoT and WSN infrastructure. These industries are shown in Table 7.2.

To effectively serve industry demands, the deployment must support the following:

- Low-latency inference to ensure rapid attack detection.
- Edge computing integration for on-site threat detection without internet dependency.
- Seamless API connectivity with existing industrial firewalls and security appliances.

7.5   Hosting Solutions

Choosing the right hosting environment is critical for ensuring the availability, scalability, and security of the deployed cybersecurity model. Table 7.3 lists the potential hosting solutions.

Table 7.3 Potential Hosting Solutions

HOSTING SOLUTION	ADVANTAGES
Heroku	Simple, managed platform for small-scale Flask-based API hosting.
AWS Lambda	Serverless, auto-scalable deployment with low operational cost.
Google Cloud AI Platform	Optimized for deploying machine learning models in production.
Microsoft Azure ML Services	Enterprise-grade cloud solutions with integrated security.
On-Premises Hosting	Provides full control and security for industries with strict data policies.

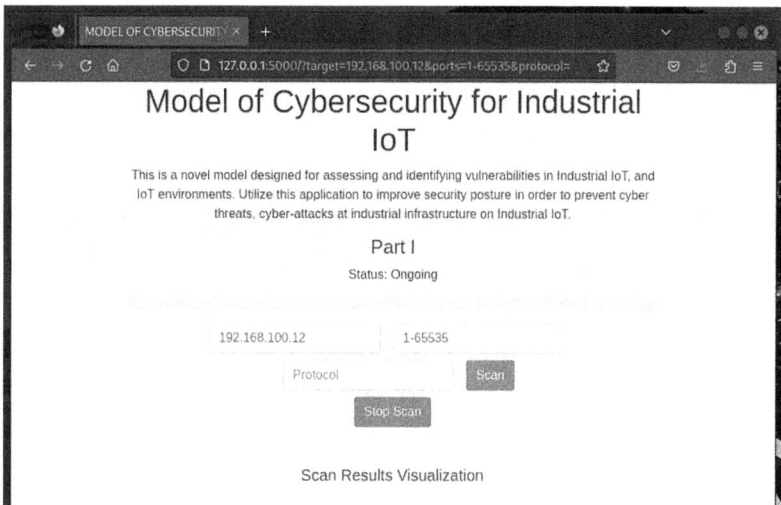

Figure 7.2 Machine learning model web interface example 1.

Cloud-based hosting (AWS, Google Cloud, or Azure) is recommended for scalability, while on-premises deployment is ideal for industries with limited regulatory compliance (Figures 7.2–7.6).

7.6 Summary

This chapter focused on the deployment of the cybersecurity model for IIoT and WSN security, including key aspects such as web interface design, API integration, real-time monitoring, and hosting solutions. By implementing a user-friendly web interface, secure API endpoints,

Model of Cybersecurity for Industrial IoT

This is a novel model designed for assessing and identifying vulnerabilities in Industrial IoT, and IoT environments. Utilize this application to improve security posture in order to prevent cyber threats, cyber-attacks at industrial infrastructure on Industrial IoT.

Part I

Status: Completed

Results saved at: static/results/Vulnerability_Scan_Results_20241104_183306.csv

192.168.100.12   1-65535   Protocol   Scan

Stop Scan

Scan Results Visualization

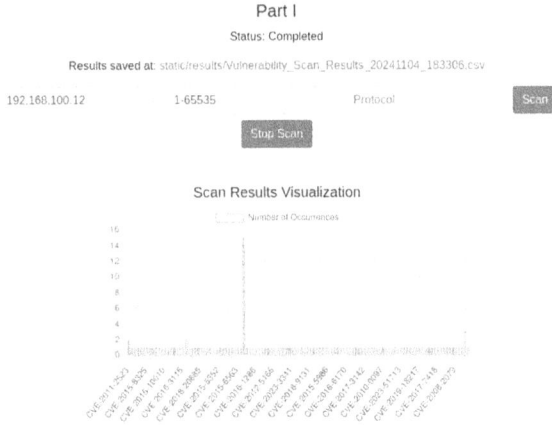

Figure 7.3 Machine learning model web interface example 2.

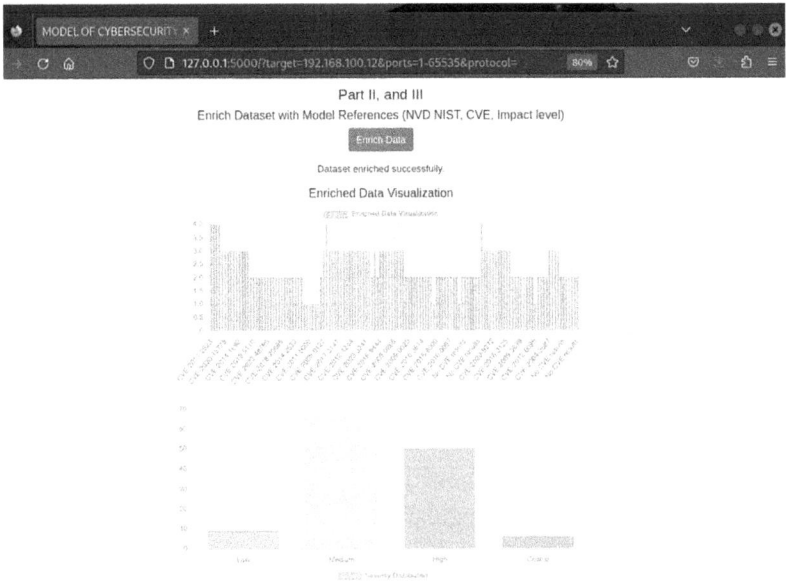

Figure 7.4 Machine learning model web interface example 3.

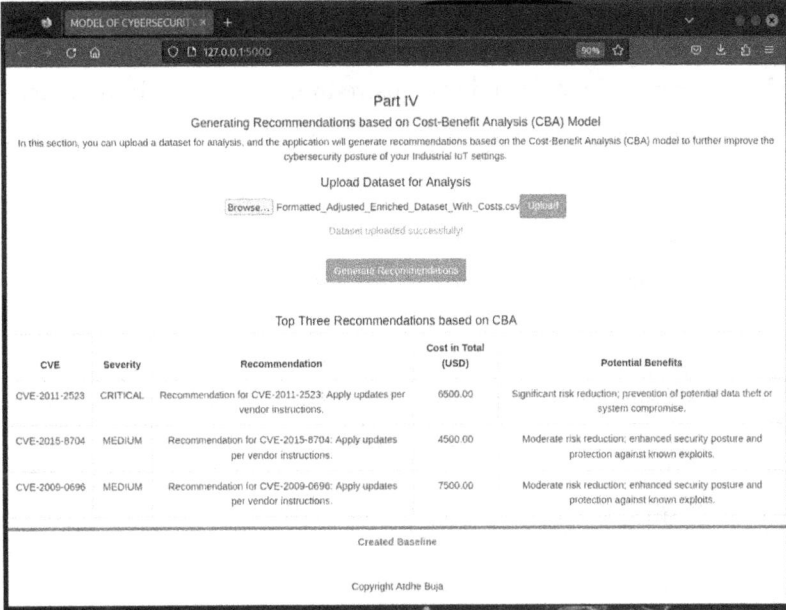

Figure 7.5   Machine learning model web interface example 4.

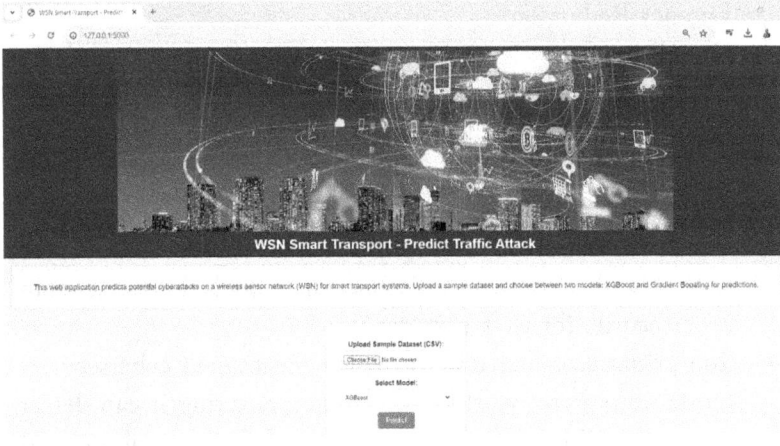

Figure 7.6   Machine learning model web interface example 5.

and real-time alerting mechanisms, the system ensures efficient cyberthreat detection and response.

Additionally, we examined cloud versus edge deployment strategies, highlighting their benefits for scalability, latency reduction, and data privacy. The deployment phase bridges the gap between model development and real-world industrial application, making cybersecurity actionable and responsive in industrial environments.

7.7   Key Terms

- Enterprise-Grade Cloud Solutions
- On-Premises Hosting
- Cloud-Based Hosting
- Scalability
- IIoT (Industrial Internet of Things)
- WSN (Wireless Sensor Network)
- Web Interface Design
- API Integration
- Real-Time Monitoring
- Hosting Solutions
- Cyberthreat Detection
- Real-Time Alerting Mechanisms
- Edge Deployment
- Latency Reduction
- Data Privacy
- Model Development
- Industrial Environments

7.8   Review Questions

1. What is the primary objective of model deployment in cybersecurity for IIoT and WSNs?
   The primary objective is to deploy the trained cybersecurity model into a real-world environment, ensuring it can detect threats, provide real-time insights, and facilitate automated responses to security breaches.

2. What are the key challenges in deploying machine learning models for cybersecurity?
   Some challenges include data privacy concerns, model interpretability, latency issues, scalability, and integration with existing security frameworks in industrial settings.

3. What best practices should be followed to ensure a successful model deployment?

   Best practices include testing the model in a simulated environment before full deployment; ensuring secure API communication to protect sensitive data; monitoring and updating the model periodically to adapt to evolving threats; implementing logging and alert mechanisms for real-time security event tracking.

4. What are the key tools and frameworks used for model deployment?

   Flask/Fast API for creating APIs, TensorFlow Serving for deploying deep learning models, Docker for containerizing the model, and Kubernetes for cloud-based hosting.

5. How does a web interface support model deployment in cybersecurity?

   A web interface provides a user-friendly dashboard to interact with the deployed model, allowing users to submit data, view real-time analytics, receive alerts, and take necessary security action.

6. What factors should be considered when designing a web interface for model deployment?

   Factors include user experience (UX), security (e.g., authentication), real-time visualization, API integration, and responsiveness for seamless access on different devices.

7. How can deployed models serve industrial applications?

   The models can monitor network traffic for anomaly detection and identify malicious activities in IIoT and WSN environments, automate threat responses to minimize cyber risks, and provide predictive analytics to prevent attacks before they occur.

8. What are the differences between edge deployment and cloud deployment for cybersecurity models?

Edge Deployment: The model runs locally on IoT/IIoT devices, reducing latency and improving security but requiring higher hardware resources.

Cloud Deployment: The model runs on cloud servers, allowing scalability, but it may introduce latency and data privacy concerns.

9. What are the common hosting solutions for deploying cybersecurity models?

   On-Premises Hosting, Cloud Hosting, and Hybrid Deployment.

10. What is API deployment, and why is it crucial in cybersecurity models?

    API deployment allows the cybersecurity model to be accessed via HTTP requests, enabling easy integration with existing security tools, automation scripts, and industry applications.

11. Why is continuous monitoring important in model deployment?

    Continuous monitoring helps detect model drift, security vulnerabilities, and performance degradation, ensuring the cybersecurity model remains effective against evolving threats.

7.9 Suggested Websites

- The ICT Academy model, where the author of this book leads, is an innovative solution leveraging machine learning (ML), artificial intelligence (AI), and cybersecurity to meet the needs of wireless sensor networks (WSN), the Internet of Things (IoT), and Industrial IoT (IIoT). [www.academyict. net/solutions/]
- NIST – AI and Cybersecurity Standards – [www.nist.gov/ cyberframework]: Guidelines on deploying AI/ML models securely in cybersecurity applications.
- OWASP – Machine Learning Security – [https://owasp.org/ www-project-ai-security-and-privacy-guide/].
- TensorFlow Serving – [www.tensorflow.org/tfx/guide/ serving].

- FastAPI – [https://fastapi.tiangolo.com/]: High-performance API for model deployment.
- Flask – [https://flask.palletsprojects.com/]: Lightweight ML API deployment.
- Docker – [www.docker.com/]: Containerized model deployment.
- MITRE ATT&CK – [https://attack.mitre.org/]: Framework for cybersecurity threats.
- IoT Security Foundation (IoTSF) – [www.iotsecurityfoundation.org/].

8

ARTIFICIAL INTELLIGENCE IN IIoT AND WSN SECURITY

8.1 Artificial Intelligence in IIoT and WSN Security

In this chapter, we deep-dive into the key role that artificial intelligence (AI) plays in advancing the cybersecurity of the Industrial Internet of Things (IIoT) and wireless sensor networks (WSNs). As the use of those technologies increased across the different industry sectors, cybersecurity became more important to maintain and enhance. AI techniques, such as machine learning (ML) and deep learning (DL), are engaged to detect anomalies, predict potential security breaches, and respond to threats in real time. By benefiting from the use of AI, IIoT and WSN systems can reach the highest levels of strength against risks, threats, and potential cyberattacks.

This chapter will investigate the current advancements in AI-driven cybersecurity measures and focus on case studies and practical applications that demonstrate the effectiveness of these technologies in protecting critical infrastructure.

Over the previous chapters, we examined and introduced the impact that machine learning models can have on and how they can enhance the cybersecurity posture of IIoT and WSN systems. Those machine learning models are trained to identify unusual patterns of behavior within IIoT and WSN infrastructures, acting as guardians against unauthorized access and data breaches. Those models, when utilized, can analyze vast amounts of data to recognize and combat advanced cyberthreats that traditional methods might fail to notice. For example, by predicting hardware failures and system malfunctions before they happen, AI not only advances operational efficiency but also mitigates the risk related to such disruptions.

DOI: 10.1201/9781003631514-8

As we dive deep, it's important to investigate how AI integrates consistently with actual cybersecurity frameworks. The combination of AI and traditional cybersecurity controls establishes a robust and adaptable protection mechanism. AI's capability to constantly learn and evolve ensures the development of dynamic security solutions that can respond to emerging threats in real time. Creative approaches, like AI-driven anomaly detection and automated response systems, advance the capabilities of existing cybersecurity protocols. By integrating AI, these frameworks become more resilient and capable of foreseeing and mitigating risks before they escalate. The continuous monitoring and analysis provided by AI make sure that the security controls are dynamic with regard to identifying vulnerabilities and attack vectors. Additionally, AI advances the predictive maintenance outlook of cybersecurity. By forecasting potential issues and facilitating preventive actions, AI contributes to the overall stability and cybersecurity of IIoT and WSN systems. This proactive approach significantly reduces downtime and prevents exploitation by threat actors (hackers or advanced persistent threats—APTs), ultimately protecting critical infrastructure.

Let's examine specific case studies and practical applications that underline the efficacy of AI-integrated cybersecurity frameworks.

- Case Study 1: AI in Power Grid Security

One important example of AI's role in cybersecurity is within the power grid sector. Power grids are critical infrastructure that needs a robust defense against cyberthreats. In this case study, AI-driven solutions are used to monitor and analyze vast amounts of data from sensors distributed over the grid. Machine learning models are trained to detect unusual patterns indicative of potential cyberattacks or system malfunctions. By identifying these anomalies in real time, AI systems can alert operators to take immediate action, preventing larger-scale disruptions. This approach not only secures the power grid against cyber threats but also advances operational efficiency through predictive maintenance.

- Case Study 2: AI in Healthcare IoT Security

The healthcare industry has increasingly applied IoT devices to monitor patient health and manage medical equipment. These devices, while beneficial, pose significant security risks. AI-integrated frameworks have been delivered to protect these IoT systems. By continuously monitoring network traffic and device behavior, AI algorithms can identify suspicious activities that may indicate a cyberattack. For instance, an AI system can detect unauthorized attempts to access patient data and automatically trigger security protocols to block such attempts. This maintains the confidentiality and integrity of sensitive medical information, thereby protecting patients and healthcare providers.

- **Practical Application: AI-Driven Anomaly Detection in Manufacturing**

Manufacturing industries have adopted IIoT technologies to optimize production processes. However, these technologies also introduce cybersecurity challenges. AI-driven anomaly detection systems are implemented to secure manufacturing networks. These systems analyze data from various sensors and machinery to identify deviations from normal operational patterns from a baseline. When anomalies are detected, AI systems can promptly initiate corrective measures, such as adjusting machine settings or isolating compromised components. This application not only advances cybersecurity but also reduces downtime and improves overall productivity.

- **Practical Application: AI in Smart City Security**

Smart cities use interconnected IoT devices to manage urban infrastructure, from traffic lights to surveillance cameras. The intricacy of these networks requires enhanced cybersecurity solutions. AI-integrated frameworks are employed to monitor and protect smart city systems. By analyzing data from multiple sources, AI can detect potential security breaches, such as unauthorized access to traffic control systems or tampering with surveillance feeds. Automated response mechanisms can then be activated to neutralize the threats, ensuring the smooth and secure operation of smart city infrastructure.

These case studies and practical applications demonstrate the transformative impact of AI on cybersecurity. By leveraging AI's capabilities, industries can achieve dynamic and resilient protection mechanisms that safeguard critical infrastructure and advance overall system security.

The role of AI in predictive maintenance is vital to advancing the cybersecurity system. Predictive maintenance uses AI algorithms to forecast potential failures in machinery and infrastructure before they happen. By analyzing historical data, sensor readings, and machine behavior, AI can predict when a component is likely to fail (as we've shown in previous chapters). This allows operators to perform maintenance proactively rather than waiting until the failure occurs, minimizing downtime and preventing unexpected breakdowns. In the context of cybersecurity, predictive maintenance has a significant role. By identifying vulnerabilities and potential points of failure in real time, AI can alert security or incident teams to potential threats before they become critical issues.

Moreover, predictive maintenance reduces the risk of threats by making sure that systems are always functioning optimally. Regular maintenance keeps software and hardware up to date, mitigating gaps that could be exploited by malicious actors. This proactive approach not only advances operational efficiency but also secures the security posture of the whole system. This unity between maintenance and cybersecurity makes sure that both physical and digital components of the critical infrastructure of IIoT and WSNs are protected. As AI technology continues to evolve, its role in predictive maintenance will become even more key, driving advancements in system security across various sectors.

8.2 Future Trends

AI's role in cybersecurity is expanded not just to detection and maintenance but also to the development of adaptive security frameworks that evolve with emerging threats. Benefiting from machine learning, these frameworks can predict and counteract advanced cyberattacks that traditional security controls may fail to address. Moreover, AI helps in automating complex security protocols, reducing the reliance on human intervention, and enhancing response times.

As industries continue to use advanced technologies within their operations, the reliance on AI for cybersecurity will only increase. From protecting patient data in healthcare to ensuring the resilience of manufacturing networks and smart city infrastructures, AI's impact is keen and far-reaching.

In summary, AI's integration within IoT security is a dynamic and ongoing process, promising significant enhancement in defending key sectors from cyberthreats. The continuous evolution of AI capabilities will shape the future of cybersecurity, driving innovation and advancing the robustness of security frameworks in various industries.

8.3   Summary

This chapter focused on the role of AI in the cybersecurity for IIoT and WSNs. As AI continues to develop, its applications in cybersecurity become increasingly advanced, providing preventive measures and adaptive responses to emerging threats. The dynamic nature of AI allows it to keep pace with the ever-evolving landscape of threats and cyberattacks, offering a robust defense mechanism that traditional security controls cannot match. Various use cases were mentioned in this chapter where the utilization of AI resulted in a well-protected business process.

AI's role in predictive maintenance extends to cybersecurity by identifying vulnerabilities and potential points of failure in real time, which helps alert security or incident teams to potential threats before they become critical issues. Future trends show that AI's role will expand to the development of adaptive security frameworks that evolve with emerging threats.

8.4   Key Terms

- AI (Artificial Intelligence)
- Predictive Maintenance
- Cybersecurity
- IIoT (Industrial Internet of Things)
- WSNs (Wireless Sensor Networks)
- Machine Learning
- Adaptive Security Frameworks
- Operational Efficiency
- Incident Teams
- Threat Detection

8.5   Review Questions

1. What is predictive maintenance and how does it benefit industrial operations?
   Predictive maintenance involves using data analysis tools and techniques to predict equipment failures before they occur. It benefits industrial operations by reducing downtime, optimizing maintenance schedules, and lowering costs.

2. Explain the importance of cybersecurity in the context of IIoT.
   Cybersecurity is crucial in IIoT as it protects sensitive data from breaches and cyberattacks, ensuring the integrity and reliability of industrial systems.

3. What is the role of WSNs in industrial applications?
   WSNs (Wireless Sensor Networks) play a vital role in industrial applications by monitoring and collecting data from various sensors, facilitating real-time decision-making and automation.

4. How can machine learning be applied to improve operational efficiency?
   Machine learning can analyze vast amounts of data to identify patterns and optimize processes, leading to improved operational efficiency and productivity.

5. What is an adaptive security framework?
   An adaptive security framework is a dynamic approach to cybersecurity that continuously evolves to address emerging threats, ensuring robust protection.

6. Identify some key benefits of enhancing operational efficiency in industrial settings.
   Enhancing operational efficiency leads to reduced costs, increased productivity, better resource utilization, and improved overall performance.

7. What are incident teams, and what role do they play in threat detection?
   Incident teams are specialized groups responsible for identifying, evaluating, and responding to security threats.

They play a crucial role in mitigating risks and protecting assets.

8. Describe some common methods used in threat detection.
   Common methods used in threat detection include anomaly detection, signature-based detection, and behavior analysis, using tools like antivirus software and intrusion detection systems.

9. How does predictive maintenance impact operational efficiency?
   Predictive maintenance impacts operational efficiency by reducing unexpected downtime, optimizing maintenance schedules, and extending the lifespan of equipment.

10. Explain how IIoT can be integrated into existing industrial systems to improve performance.
    IIoT can be integrated into existing systems by implementing smart sensors and devices that collect and analyze data, providing insights for better decision-making and automation.

11. What are some challenges associated with implementing machine learning in industrial environments?
    Challenges include managing large volumes of data, ensuring data quality, integrating with existing systems, and the need for skilled personnel to develop and maintain machine learning models.

8.6   Suggested Websites

- NIST – AI and Cybersecurity Standards – [www.nist.gov/cyberframework]: Guidelines on deploying AI/ML models securely in cybersecurity applications.
- OWASP – Machine Learning Security – [https://owasp.org/www-project-ai-security-and-privacy-guide/].
- IBM – Artificial Intelligence (AI) Cybersecurity – [www.ibm.com/ai-cybersecurity].
- Microsoft – What Is AI for Cybersecurity? – [www.microsoft.com/en-us/security/business/security-101/what-is-ai-for-cybersecurity].
- CISA – CISA's Roadmap for Artificial Intelligence – [www.cisa.gov/ai].

9

RESEARCH INSIGHTS

9.1 Research Insights

In this chapter, we discuss the complex dynamics of Industrial Internet of Things (IIoT) and wireless sensor network (WSN) security. This investigation unearths significant insights into the actual research trends, vulnerabilities, and novel strategies used to mitigate risks. By investigating real-world use cases and frameworks, we are able to focus on offering a thorough understanding of the multilayered security landscape in IIoT and WSN systems. So, previous chapters explored the role of machine learning and artificial intelligence in predicting and preventing security breaches, highlighting case studies where these technologies have been successfully implemented. Furthermore, the discussion extends to the importance of interoperability among different systems and devices, underscoring how seamless integration can enhance overall security posture. This knowledge is essential for both researchers and practitioners aiming to design robust security frameworks for future applications.

Over the research work within this book, the designing and deployment of a machine learning-based cybersecurity model for IIoT and WSN environments provided valuable insights into the technical and practical aspects of securing smart industrial systems. A vital insight is the importance of data preprocessing and feature engineering in achieving accurate and meaningful predictions. The model's effectiveness was directly related to the quality and balance of the dataset, as well as the relevance of the selected features that reflect real-world attack behaviors.

Another fact is the use of visualization in understanding the highlighted attack patterns and advancing explainability. Confusion

DOI: 10.1201/9781003631514-9

matrices, ROC curves, and heatmaps not only supported model evaluation but also provided stakeholders with a clear view of the model's decision-making process. Moreover, deploying the model via APIs and integrating it into a web-based interface exhibited the feasibility of using AI/ML in practical, real-time IIoT/WSN systems, bridging the gap between research and industry application.

9.2   Lessons Learned

This research work reveals key lessons learned that can be offered to future research and development in cybersecurity for IIoT and WSN environments. First, data imbalance is a constant challenge—many real-world cybersecurity datasets contain far fewer attack instances than normal operations. This imbalance must be addressed through stratified sampling or anomaly detection approaches. Second, model generalization is just as important as accuracy.

A model that performs well in one scenario may fail in another if not trained on various and representative data. It's important to build models that are resilient in the face of evolving attack strategies and can adapt to new patterns with minimal retraining.

Finally, deployment is not the end of the process—it's the beginning of continuous monitoring and maintenance. Models must be monitored for leaks, retrained as new data arrives, and integrated with security operations so that they remain effective. Underlining interdisciplinary collaboration between data scientists, network engineers, and security professionals is also key to ensuring successful adoption.

9.3   Emerging Challenges in IIoT and WSN Security

As IIoT and WSN systems continue to grow in intricacy and scale, new challenges are emerging in the realm of cybersecurity. One significant issue is the increasing advancement of cyberthreats, which are becoming harder to detect with traditional security methods. Attackers are now utilizing AI themselves to bypass detection systems, making it imperative to adopt adaptive and intelligent defense mechanisms.

Another pressing issue is the resource limitation of IIoT and WSN nodes. These devices often have minimal computational power and memory, making it difficult to deploy complex security algorithms directly on the edge. This creates a need for lightweight ML models or hybrid edge-cloud architectures that can offload computation while maintaining low latency.

Additionally, data privacy and regulatory compliance are growing concerns. With the rise of global standards like GDPR (General Data Protection Regulation) and sector-specific regulations, security solutions must be designed to respect data sovereignty and ensure secure communication, storage, and processing of sensitive data. Looking forward, addressing zero-trust architectures (ZTAs), decentralized learning, and real-time threat intelligence sharing will be critical in shaping the next generation of cybersecurity in IIoT and WSN infrastructures.

9.4 Summary

This chapter covers the key findings and insights from the research on cybersecurity in IIoT and WSN systems. By investigating the layered complexity of data imbalance, model generalization, and deployment challenges, this work highlights the need for adaptive methodologies and interdisciplinary collaboration. As the IIoT and WSN domains evolve, so too must our security frameworks, embracing intelligent, resource-efficient, and regulation-compliant approaches to protect against the ever-advancing landscape of cyberthreats.

By integrating AI-driven analytics and proactive threat detection systems, security frameworks can foresee and neutralize threats before they escalate. Continuous education and training for cybersecurity professionals, along with fostering innovation through partnerships between academia and industry, are essential to maintaining robust security postures in IIoT and WSN systems.

9.5 Key Terms

- IIoT (Industrial Internet of Things)
- WSNs (Wireless Sensor Networks)
- Cybersecurity
- AI (Artificial Intelligence)
- ML (Machine Learning)

- Data Imbalance
- Model Generalization
- Deployment Challenges
- Adaptive Defense Mechanisms
- Resource Limitation
- Edge-Cloud Architectures
- Data Privacy
- GDPR (General Data Protection Regulation)
- Zero-Trust Architectures (ZTAs)
- Decentralized Learning
- Threat Intelligence Sharing

9.6   Review Questions

1. What are the primary deployment challenges in modern network security?

   Deployment challenges include scalability, integration with existing infrastructure, and ensuring compliance with evolving regulations.

2. How do adaptive defense mechanisms enhance cybersecurity?
   Adaptive defense mechanisms dynamically adjust security measures in response to emerging threats, improving resilience and response times.

3. What limitations do resources impose on cybersecurity initiatives?

   Limited resources, such as budget, personnel, and technology, can hinder the implementation and maintenance of robust security measures.

4. What are edge-cloud architectures, and how do they benefit data processing?

   Edge-cloud architectures distribute data processing between local devices (edge) and centralized cloud servers, enhancing efficiency and reducing latency.

5. Why is data privacy crucial in cybersecurity, and what measures are taken to protect it?

Data privacy ensures that sensitive information is protected from unauthorized access. Measures include encryption, access controls, and data anonymization.

6. What is GDPR, and how does it impact data management practices?
   GDPR is a regulation that mandates strict data protection and privacy for individuals within the EU, influencing how organizations handle personal data.

7. How do Zero-Trust Architectures (ZTAs) improve security postures?
   ZTA eliminates implicit trust within a network and requires continuous verification of every user and device, thereby reducing potential attack surfaces.

8. What is decentralized learning, and what advantages does it offer for security?
   Decentralized learning involves distributing the learning process across multiple nodes, enhancing privacy and reducing the risk of data breaches.

9. How does threat intelligence sharing contribute to cybersecurity efforts?
   Threat intelligence sharing allows organizations to collectively analyze threats, improving detection and response capabilities across the community.

10. What role does continuous monitoring play in adaptive defense mechanisms?
    Continuous monitoring provides real-time insights into network activities, enabling prompt detection and mitigation of threats.

11. What strategies can be employed to overcome resource limitations in cybersecurity?
    Strategies include prioritizing critical assets, leveraging automation, and collaborating with external partners to maximize available resources.

9.7   Suggested Websites

- National Institute of Standards and Technology (NIST) Cybersecurity Framework – [www.nist.gov/cyberframework].
- Cybersecurity & Infrastructure Security Agency (CISA) – [www.cisa.gov].
- European Union Agency for Cybersecurity (ENISA) – [https://enisa.europa.eu].
- Center for Internet Security (CIS) – [www.cisecurity.org].
- Zero Trust Architecture (ZTA) – [https://nvlpubs.nist.gov/nistpubs/specialpublications/NIST.SP.800-207.pdf].

10

THE PATH AHEAD

10.1 The Way Ahead

As cybersecurity attacks progress to evolve with the increased expansion of Industrial IoT and wireless sensor networks, the way forward needs proactive, intelligent, and adaptable security mechanisms. The research and development work presented in this book offers a foundation for building machine learning model detection systems, but it is only the beginning. Future directions must involve continuous data collection, real-time adaptation, and integration with automated response systems.

The way ahead also includes enhancing autonomous security frameworks—systems that can not only detect and classify attacks but also recommend or initiate security measures with minimal human intervention. Incorporating technologies such as federated learning, self-healing networks, digital twins for cybersecurity simulation, and AI-enhanced threat intelligence will be central to the evolution of this field. Furthermore, collaboration between academia, industry, and policymakers will be essential to define secure, scalable, and interoperable frameworks tailored to IIoT/WSN deployments.

10.2 Learning More

For researchers, practitioners, and students interested in expanding their knowledge, various pathways provide deeper exploration into the themes discussed in this book.

- Cybersecurity courses and certifications such as CompTIA Security+, CISSP, and Certified IoT Security Practitioner (CIoTSP) provide foundational and specialized knowledge.

DOI: 10.1201/9781003631514-10   117

- Engaging in hands-on projects using platforms like GNS3, Wireshark, and MITRE ATT&CK helps reinforce theoretical concepts with practical skills.
- Exploring open-source datasets for IIoT and WSN security and participating in cybersecurity competitions (e.g., CTFs and hackathons) foster innovation and learning.
- Reading current whitepapers, standards (e.g., NIST, ENISA), and industry reports helps maintain an up-to-date perspective on emerging threats and defensive strategies.
- The learning journey in cybersecurity is continuous, and as threat landscapes change, staying updated and engaged through community forums, professional networks, and open-source collaboration is key to long-term growth.

10.3 Summary

In addition to formal education, practical experience is valuable. Internships with leading cybersecurity firms or governmental agencies can provide real-world insights and training that are vital for understanding complex security environments. Networking with professionals at conferences and seminars can open doors to collaborations and mentorship opportunities that can significantly enhance one's career trajectory.

Additionally, staying informed on the latest cybersecurity trends and emerging technologies through subscribing to journals like *IEEE Xplore* or the *Journal of Cybersecurity* ensures that one's knowledge remains current. Utilizing social media platforms such as LinkedIn to follow thought leaders and participate in discussions can also be beneficial.

Finally, contributing to open-source security projects or writing blogs about personal research findings can help build a professional profile that stands out in the cybersecurity community.

10.4 Suggested Websites

- NIST Cybersecurity Framework – [www.nist.gov/cyberframework]: Guidelines and best practices.
- MITRE ATT&CK – [https://attack.mitre.org]: Knowledge base of adversarial tactics and techniques.

- IoT Security Foundation (IoTSF) – [www.iotsecurityfoundation.org]: Standards and guidance for IoT security.
- Cybersecurity & Infrastructure Security Agency (CISA) – [www.cisa.gov]: National threat alerts and tools.
- Kaggle – [www.kaggle.com]: Open-source datasets and notebooks.
- Scikit-learn Documentation – [https://scikit-learn.org]: ML library for model development.
- TensorFlow Security Guidelines – [https://generativeai.pub/tensorflow-tutorial-17-tensorflow-security-best-practices-for-secure-model-training-b2fbf84079d6]: AI model development and secure deployment.
- GNS3 – [www.gns3.com]: Network simulation platform for security testing.
- Google Cloud AI & ML – [https://cloud.google.com/products/ai]: Model deployment and monitoring in production.
- NICCS Certified Internet of Things Security Practitioner (CIoTSP) – [https://niccs.cisa.gov/education-training/catalog/united-training-commercial-llc/certified-internet-things-security].

Bibliography

M. Al-Hawawreh, F. den Hartog, and E. Sitnikova, "Targeted Ransomware: A New Cyber Threat to Edge System of Brownfield Industrial Internet of Things," *IEEE Internet of Things Journal*, vol. 6, no. 4, pp. 7137–7151, Aug. 2019, doi: 10.1109/jiot.2019.2914390.

Britannica, "Information System," 2022. [Online]. Available: www.britannica.com/topic/information-system.

BRM. Applied Research. https://research-methodology.net/research-methodology/research-types/applied-research/.

A. Buja, "Cybersecurity of Industrial Internet of Things (IIoT)," May 2025, doi: 10.1201/9781003383253.

A. Buja, M. Apostolova, and A. Luma, "Enhancing Cyber Security in Industrial Internet of Things Systems: An Experimental Assessment," 2023 12th Mediterranean Conference on Embedded Computing (MECO), pp. 1–5, Jun. 2023, doi: 10.1109/meco58584.2023.10155100.

A. Buja, M. Apostolova, and A. Luma, "A Model Proposal for Enhancing Cyber Security in Industrial IoT Environments," *Indonesian Journal of Electrical Engineering and Computer Science*, vol. 36, no. 1, p. 231, Oct. 2024, doi: 10.11591/ijeecs.v36.i1.pp231-241.

A. Buja, M. Apostolova, and A. Luma, "A Model Proposal of Cybersecurity for the IIoT: Enhancing IIoT Cybersecurity through Machine Learning and Deep Learning Techniques," *Advances in Artificial Intelligence and Machine Learning*, vol. 04, no. 03, pp. 2408–2415, 2024, doi: 10.54364/aaiml.2024.43140.

A. Buja, M. Apostolova, A. Luma, and Y. Januzaj, "Cyber Security Standards for the Industrial Internet of Things (IIoT) – A Systematic Review," 2022 International Congress on Human-Computer Interaction, *Optimization and Robotic Applications (HORA)*, pp. 1–6, Jun. 2022, doi: 10.1109/hora55278.2022.9799870.

A. Buja, M. Pacolli, D. Bajrami, P. Polstra, and A. Mutoh, "Enhancing IoT Security Development and Evaluation of a Predictive Machine Learning Model for Attack Detection," *Advances in Artificial Intelligence and Machine Learning*, vol. 04, no. 03, pp. 2490–2498, 2024, doi: 10.54364/aaiml.2024.43145.

A. Buja, M. Pacolli, D. Bajrami, P. Polstra, and A. Mutoh, "Innovative Machine Learning Model Design for Predictive IoT Security Attacks," *Advances in Artificial Intelligence and Machine Learning*, vol. 04, no. 02, pp. 2394–2407, 2024, doi: 10.54364/aaiml.2024.42139.

A. Buja, M. Pacolli, D. Bajrami, P. Polstra, and A. Mutoh, "Time-Series Analysis on AIDE IoT Attack Data Unraveling Trends and Patterns for Enhanced Security," *Advances in Artificial Intelligence and Machine Learning*, vol. 04, no. 02, pp. 2233–2243, 2024, doi: 10.54364/aaiml.2024.42128.

CompTia, "What Is Cybersecurity?," [Online]. Available: www.comptia.org/content/articles/what-is-cybersecurity.

A. A. Cook, G. Misirli, and Z. Fan, "Anomaly Detection for IoT Time-Series Data: A Survey," *IEEE Internet of Things Journal*, vol. 7, no. 7, pp. 6481–6494, Jul. 2020, doi: 10.1109/jiot.2019.2958185.

Cybersecurity CISA. The Colonial Pipeline Ransomware Attack: A Case Study on the Financial Impact of Cyberattacks. Retrieved from www.cisa.gov/news-events/news/attack-colonial-pipeline-what-weve-learned-what-weve-done-over-past-two-years2021.

S. Dalal et al., "Next-Generation Cyber Attack Prediction for IoT Systems: Leveraging Multi-Class SVM and Optimized CHAID Decision Tree," *Journal of Cloud Computing*, vol. 12, no. 1, Sep. 2023, doi: 10.1186/s13677-023-00517-4.

EC-Council. Five Methodologies That Can Improve Your Penetration Testing ROI. www.eccouncil.org/cybersecurity-exchange/penetration-testing/penetration-testing-methodology-improve-pen-testing-roi/

European Union Agency for Cybersecurity (ENISA). Ransomware Attacks on the Rise. Retrieved from www.enisa.europa.eu/news/enisa-news/enisa-threat-landscape-2020.

Gartner, "Gartner Glossary," Gartner, [Online]. Available: www.gartner.com/en/information-technology/glossary/internet-of-things.

T. Gueye, Y. Wang, M. Rehman, R. T. Mushtaq, and S. Zahoor, "A Novel Method to Detect Cyber-Attacks in IoT/IIoT Devices on the Modbus Protocol Using Deep Learning," *Cluster Computing*, vol. 26, no. 5, pp. 2947–2973, Jun. 2023, doi: 10.1007/s10586-023-04028-4.

R. Z. Haider, B. Aslam, H. Abbas, and Z. Iqbal, "C2-Eye: Framework for Detecting Command and Control (C2) Connection of Supply Chain Attacks," *International Journal of Information Security*, vol. 23, no. 4, pp. 2531–2545, Apr. 2024, doi: 10.1007/s10207-024-00850-y.

S. Haque, F. El-Moussa, N. Komninos, and R. Muttukrishnan, "A Systematic Review of Data-Driven Attack Detection Trends in IoT," *Sensors*, vol. 23, no. 16, p. 7191, Aug. 2023, doi: 10.3390/s23167191.

A. Huc and D. Trcek, "Anomaly Detection in IoT Networks: From Architectures to Machine Learning Transparency," *IEEE Access*, vol. 9, pp. 60607–60616, 2021, doi: 10.1109/access.2021.3073785.

ISACA. COBIT: Control Objectives for Information and Related Technology. 2021. Retrieved from www.isaca.org/cobit

ISO. ISO 27001:2013 – Information Technology – Security Techniques – Information Security Management Systems – Requirements. 2021. Retrieved from www.iso.org/standard/64513.html

O. Jullian, B. Otero, E. Rodriguez, N. Gutierrez, H. Antona, and R. Canal, "Deep-Learning Based Detection for Cyber-Attacks in IoT Networks: A Distributed Attack Detection Framework," *Journal of Network and Systems Management*, vol. 31, no. 2, Feb. 2023, doi: 10.1007/s10922-023-09722-7.

A. Khan and C. Cotton, "Efficient Attack Detection in IoT Devices Using Feature Engineering-Less Machine Learning," *International Journal of Computer Science and Information Technology*, vol. 14, no. 6, pp. 47–64, Dec. 2022, doi: 10.5121/ijcsit.2022.14605.

F. Li, A. Shinde, Y. Shi, J. Ye, X.-Y. Li, and W. Song, "System Statistics Learning-Based IoT Security: Feasibility and Suitability," *IEEE Internet of Things Journal*, vol. 6, no. 4, pp. 6396–6403, Aug. 2019, doi: 10.1109/jiot.2019.2897063.

McKinsey.com. A Manufacturer's Guide to Scaling Industrial IoT. www.mckinsey.com/capabilities/mckinsey-digital/our-insights/a-manufacturers-guide-to-generating-value-at-scale-with-industrial-iot

McKinsey.com. Cybersecurity for the IoT: How Trust Can Unlock Value. www.mckinsey.com/industries/technology-media-and-telecommunications/our-insights/cybersecurity-for-the-iot-how-trust-can-unlock-value

McKinsey.com. Digital Twins: The Next Frontier of Factory Optimization. www.mckinsey.com/capabilities/operations/our-insights/digital-twins-the-next-frontier-of-factory-optimization

McKinsey.com. Insights on the Internet of Things. www.mckinsey.com/featured-insights/internet-of-things/our-insights

McKinsey.com. Leveraging Industrial IoT and Advanced Technologies for Digital Transformation. https://shorturl.at/EiecQ

McKinsey.com. McKinsey Technology Trends Outlook. 2024. www.mckinsey.com/capabilities/mckinsey-digital/our-insights/the-top-trends-in-tech

B. K. Mohanta, D. Jena, U. Satapathy, and S. Patnaik, "Survey on IoT Security: Challenges and Solution Using Machine Learning, Artificial Intelligence and Blockchain Technology," *Internet of Things*, vol. 11, p. 100227, Sep. 2020, doi: 10.1016/j.iot.2020.100227.

National Institute of Standards and Technology (NIST). Cybersecurity Framework. Retrieved from www.nist.gov/cyberframework

C. Nielsen, M. Lund, M. Montemari, F. Paolone, M. Massaro, and J. Dumay, "Applied Research Methodology." In *Business Models*, pp. 16–21, Nov. 2018. Taylor & Francis. doi: 10.4324/9781351232272-2.

NIST, "Glossary Information Technology (IT)," NIST, [Online]. Available: https://csrc.nist.gov/glossary/term/information_technology.

NVD NIST. National Vulnerability Database. https://nvd.nist.gov/vuln

OSINT Framework. OSINT Framework .https://osintframework.com/

OWASP. Penetration Testing Methodologies. https://owasp.org/www-proj ect-web-security-testing-guide/latest/3-The_OWASP_Testing_Framew ork/1-Penetration_Testing_Methodologies

S. Qin, L. Chen, Y. Luo, and G. Tao, "Multiview Graph Contrastive Learning for Multivariate Time-Series Anomaly Detection in IoT," *IEEE Internet of Things Journal*, vol. 10, no. 24, pp. 22401–22414, Dec. 2023, doi: 10.1109/jiot.2023.3303946.

T. Rajmohan, P. H. Nguyen, and N. Ferry, "A Decade of Research on Patterns and Architectures for IoT security," *Cybersecurity*, vol. 5, no. 1, Jan. 2022, doi: 10.1186/s42400-021-00104-7.

M. Raparthy et al., "Predictive Maintenance in IoT Devices Using Time Series Analysis and Deep Learning," *Dandao Xuebao/Journal of Ballistics*, vol. 35, no. 3, pp. 01–10, Dec. 2023, doi: 10.52783/dxjb.v35.113.

P. Rosenzweig, *Cybersecurity and Cyberwar: What Everyone Needs to Know* (Oxford University Press, 2014).

M. Saied, S. Guirguis, and M. Madbouly, "A Comparative Analysis of Using Ensemble Trees for Botnet Detection and Classification in IoT," *Scientific Reports*, vol. 13, no. 1, Dec. 2023, doi: 10.1038/s41598-023-48681-6.

T. B. Seong, V. Ponnusamy, N. Zaman Jhanjhi, R. Annur, and M. N. Talib, "A Comparative Analysis on Traditional Wired Datasets and the Need for Wireless Datasets for IoT Wireless Intrusion Detection," *Indonesian Journal of Electrical Engineering and Computer Science*, vol. 22, no. 2, p. 1165, May 2021, doi: 10.11591/ijeecs.v22.i2.pp1165-1176.

Trend Micro. Advanced Persistent Threat (APT). Definition – Trend Micro USA. Retrieved from www.trendmicro.com/en_my/what-is.html

S. O. Uwagbole, W. J. Buchanan, and L. Fan, "Applied Machine Learning Predictive Analytics to SQL Injection Attack Detection and Prevention," *2017 IFIP/IEEE Symposium on Integrated Network and Service Management (IM)*, pp. 1087–1090, May 2017, doi: 10.23919/inm.2017.7987433.

T. Zhukabayeva, A. Buja, and M. Pacolli, "Evaluating Security Mechanisms for Wireless Sensor Networks in IoT and IIoT," *Journal of Robotics and Control (JRC)*, vol. 5, p. 21683, May 2024, doi: 10.18196/jrc.v5i4.21683.

T. Zhukabayeva, A. Buja, M. Pacolli, and Y. Mardenov, "Detecting Network Security Incidents in Wireless Sensor Networks Using Machine Learning," *Indonesian Journal of Electrical Engineering and Computer Science*, vol. 37, no. 3, p. 1650, Mar. 2025, doi: 10.11591/ijeecs.v37.i3.pp1650-1660.

For Product Safety Concerns and Information please contact our EU
representative GPSR@taylorandfrancis.com
Taylor & Francis Verlag GmbH, Kaufingerstraße 24, 80331 München, Germany

www.ingramcontent.com/pod-product-compliance
Lightning Source LLC
Chambersburg PA
CBHW070735220326
41598CB00024BA/3432